ST. MARY'S COLLEGE OF MARYLAND LIBRARY
ST. M

P9-ARV-698

4.87 -B&T 9-66 (Perkins)

Ancient Peoples and Places

NEW GRANGE

General Editor

DR GLYN DANIEL

ABOUT THE AUTHORS

Sean P. Ó Ríordáin was born in Cork in 1905 and died in Dublin in 1957. At the early age of thirty-one he became Professor of Archaeology in University College, Cork, and, seven years later, moved to the Chair of Archaeology in University College, Dublin, which he held until his death. Although only in his early fifties when he died, he was well established as the doyen of Irish archaeology, and was widely known outside the British Isles for his work at Cush, Garranes, Lough Gur and Tara, as well as for his friendship, hospitality, enthusiasm, and good company.

Glyn Daniel was born in South Wales in 1914, and since 1932 (apart from his war service in the Photographic Intelligence branch of the R.A.F.) has been in Cambridge where he is a Fellow of St John's College, and a Lecturer in Archaeology in the University. His main interests are megalithic monuments, prehistoric art, and the history of archaeology, and he has written books on all these subjects. He is Editor of ANTIQUITY *and General Editor of the series* ANCIENT PEOPLES AND PLACES, *in which this book appears. Close friends, Dr Daniel and Professor Ó Ríordáin conceived this book together, did the necessary fieldwork together, and together wrote two-thirds of it before the latter's untimely death.*

Ancient Peoples and Places

NEW GRANGE

AND THE BEND OF THE BOYNE

Sean P. Ó Ríordáin

Glyn Daniel

70 PHOTOGRAPHS
23 LINE DRAWINGS
8 MAPS

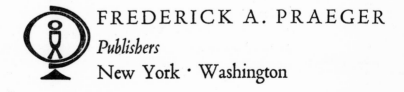

FREDERICK A. PRAEGER

Publishers

New York · Washington

THIS IS VOLUME FORTY IN THE SERIES
Ancient Peoples and Places
GENERAL EDITOR: DR. GLYN DANIEL

BOOKS THAT MATTER

*Published in the United States of America
in 1964 by Frederick A. Praeger, Inc.
Publishers, 111 Fourth Avenue
New York 3, N.Y.
All rights reserved
© Glyn Daniel 1964
Library of Congress Catalog Card Number: 64-22496
Printed in Great Britain*

16505

CONTENTS

LIST OF ILLUSTRATIONS   7

PREFACE   12

I   NEW GRANGE   15
    The Bend of the Boyne   15
    Megaliths and chamber tombs   20
    New Grange today   26
    New Grange in history   30
    The original New Grange   48
    The stones   50

II   THE ART OF NEW GRANGE   51

III   DOWTH AND KNOWTH   65
    Dowth   65
    Knowth   72
    The Bend of the Boyne   77

IV   THE IRISH AND BRITISH
    PASSAGE GRAVES   91
    Ireland: the southern tombs   93
    Ireland: tombs west of the Boyne   99
    Ireland: tombs north of Dublin   101
    Passage Graves in Great Britain   102
    Grave goods   109

The Abbé Breuil and Irish megalithic art III

Motifs in the art 114

V CULTURAL AND CHRONOLOGICAL
CONTEXTS 118

BIBLIOGRAPHICAL NOTE 154

TRAVEL NOTE 157

SOURCES OF ILLUSTRATIONS 158

THE PLATES 161

NOTES ON THE PLATES 209

INDEX 215

ILLUSTRATIONS

PLATES   1   New Grange from the air
2   New Grange from the ground
3   The stone circle
4   Construction of mound
5   Decorated lintel stone above entrance
6   Decorated stone at entrance
7   Looking up passage from entrance
8   Stone R 12 in passage
9   The passage, looking back from chamber
10   Roof of central chamber
11   The south side chamber
12   Stone basins in north side chamber
13, 14   Stone R 18—technique of decoration
15   Decoration on stone, south side chamber
16   Triskele spiral
17   Detail of decoration on stone L 19
18   General view of stone L 19
19   Stone R 21 with details of ribbing
20   Decoration on stone L 22
21   Decoration on stone C 16
22   Decoration on stone R 21
23   Back stone of chamber
24   The so-called fir-tree man
25   Coffey's 'ship'
26   Decorated lintel above stone C 2

7

PLATES 27 Decoration on stone C 2

28 General view of decoration on underside of capstone, north side chamber

29 Detail of roofing, north side chamber

30 Detail of decoration on roofing stone, north side chamber

31 Edge of decorated stone over C 14

32 Decorated corbel over C 15

33 The passage, looking out from the chamber

34 Decorated lintel above R 20 and 21

35 Decorated kerb-stone

36 Loughcrew Passage Grave cemetery

37 Knowth from the air

38 Dowth from the air

39 Southern main chamber, Dowth

40 Entrance to side chamber from south main chamber, Dowth

41 End of passage from main chamber, Dowth

42 Detail of decoration, north chamber, Dowth

43, 44 Decorated stones in kerb circle, Dowth

45 Entrance to south chamber and kerb-stone, Dowth

46 Outline plan on top of mound, Dowth

47 North recess of north chamber, Dowth

48, 49 Decorated kerb-stones, Knowth

50 Tumulus B near New Grange

51 Henge monument O near New Grange

52 Circular earthworks north-west of New Grange

53 Circular earthworks north of Knowth

54 Dowth henge circle from the air

PLATES 55 Modern megalithic sculpture

56, 57 Art on stones, Loughcrew

58–60 Decorated lintels, Fourknocks

61 Decorated stone, Knockmany

62 Decorated stone, Fourknocks

63 Decorated stones, Seskillgreen

64 Decorated stone, Fourknocks

65 The Clear Island stone

66 Decorated stone near Loughcrew

67, 68 Decorated stones from tombs at Loughcrew

69 Stone 22, Barclodiad y Gawres

70 Decorated stone, Gavrinis

FIGURES 1 *Map of Ireland locating New Grange, p. 17*

2 *Map: The Bend of the Boyne and surrounding district, p. 18*

3 *Types of megalithic tombs in north-western Europe, p. 23*

4 *Plan of the mound, New Grange, p. 27*

5 *South-North section, New Grange, p. 27*

6 *Plan of chamber, New Grange, p. 28*

7 *Sections through chambers and passage, New Grange, p. 29*

8 *Drawing by Anstis of stone found near New Grange, p. 36*

9 *Drawing by Anstis of New Grange, p. 37*

10 *Stone L 19, New Grange, p. 56*

11 *Underside of capstone, north side chamber, New Grange, p. 62*

12 *Stones a and b in kerb circle, New Grange, p. 63*

9

FIGURES

13*a*   *Plan and section, Dowth, p. 68*

13*b*   *Plan of chambers, Dowth, p. 69*

14   *'Ship markings', Dowth, p. 72*

15   *Macalister's plan of Knowth, p. 74*

16   *Decorated stone, Knowth, after Macalister, p. 75*

17   *Kerb-stones, Knowth, after Macalister, p. 76*

18   *Sketch by Anstis of monument near New Grange, p. 78*

19   *Sketches by Anstis of sites near New Grange, p. 79*

20   *Map: Mounds and earthworks in the Bend of the Boyne, p. 81*

21   *Plan of site K, New Grange, p. 85*

22   *Plan of smaller monument, Knowth, p. 86*

23   *Plan of Towneley Hall site, p. 89*

24   *Map: Distribution of Passage Graves in Ireland, p. 92*

25   *Map: Distribution of Passage Grave art in Ireland, p. 94*

26   *Plan of Fourknocks I, p. 96*

27   *Decorated stones at Seefin, p. 99*

28   *Map: Distribution of Passage Graves in the British Isles, p. 103*

29   *Map: Distribution of Passage Grave art in the British Isles, p. 107*

30   *Classification of motifs in Irish Passage Grave, art p. 115*

31   *Map: Sites in Iberia and southern France, after Blance, p. 135*

for
GABRIEL

Preface

THE DEATH of Professor Sean ÓRíordáin in his early fifties in 1957 was not only a tragic loss to his family and friends, to the National University of Ireland, and to the cause of archaeology in and outside Ireland; it was a special private loss to the 'Ancient Peoples and Places' series. He had been invited to give the Rhind Lectures in Edinburgh and was planning them at the time of his death; he had agreed to rewrite them as a volume on Pre-Christian Ireland for the series. It was to tell the story of Ireland up to the volume on Early Christian Ireland in the series written, at his suggestion, by his friends and pupils Máire and Liam de Paor.

ÓRíordáin had always been interested in the great tombs of the Bend of the Boyne, which are one of the glories of Ireland —ancient or modern. For years he sent his students to New Grange and Dowth to describe the monuments, and it was his idea to collate the independent descriptions of these indepen-dent observers into a catalogue of the mural megalithic art in the Bend of the Boyne. He it was too who organized the photo-graphy of all the visible art by a wide variety of photographers. I urged him to publish the best of these remarkable photographs as a monograph on New Grange which would supersede Coffey's book published in 1912. He remained hesitant, but when the 'Ancient Peoples and Places' series was launched, said he would do such a book in the series if I would be his co-author. 'After all,' he said over lunch in Mrs Macken's hospitable inn where I now, seven years later, write these words alone, 'New Grange is one of the most important ancient places in Europe.'

We planned the book and wrote nearly two thirds of it in 1956 and 1957. Since his death various circumstances have contributed to the delay in its completion. Now it is done and offered as the document we had in mind seven years ago, but brought up-to-date. Chapters I, II and III were nearly complete in draft when he died. The rest is based on notes and draft passages agreed to by us both; but it must be clear to readers that this book while planned by ÓRíordáin and Daniel, is produced for the printer by Daniel using facts and data published since 1957. I can only say that had it been ÓRíordáin who had survived and Daniel who had died I would have been happy at the use of 'we' to the end of the book. We did go over with care what we intended to say and our views on the dating of Carn H at Loughcrew are what we agreed years ago.

When—and if—he finished digging at Tara, Sean ÓRíordáin hoped he might dig at New Grange—not only in the tomb but in the circular structures, possibly henge monuments, near by. This book was a sort of survey preparatory to excavation. Now the excavations he never conducted at New Grange are being done by his pupil and successor at Cork, Professor M. J. O'Kelly. Professor O'Kelly was a great friend of both of us and I have been delighted to visit his splendidly conducted and most successful excavations at New Grange in 1962 and 1963. While he has been ready to place at my disposal the results of his discoveries—many of them sensational and of the most outstanding importance—it seemed to me that this book should not anticipate his own publication.

The archaeologist and general reader will then have in a few years' time three documents about these great tombs: Coffey's book of 1912, the ÓRíordáin-Daniel book of 1964, and the definitive report of the O'Kelly excavations of 1962–4. This last document will of course not only add a very great deal to our knowledge but may well prove wrong many of our speculations; but at least we are supplying him with a contemporary document to alter. I have been careful not to include in this revised text anything I have learned from visiting New Grange with Professor O'Kelly during his excavations; this is New Grange *et al.* pre-Kelly, but post-Coffey—and, as it sadly turns out, post-ÓRíordáin.

When my co-author was alive we never discussed the dedication of this book, and it is the surviving author who dedicates it to his co-author's widow in his memory. She is a distinguished sculptress and we set her the task of reproducing some of the carvings at New Grange with stone chisels; one of her results is reproduced here (Plate 55). Gabriel ÓRíordáin is thus perhaps the only megalithic artist whose name is known.

G.D.

The Conyngham Arms,
Slane. 1st October, 1963.

CHAPTER I

New Grange

THE BEND OF THE BOYNE

Tᴴᴱ ɢʀᴇᴀᴛ ᴄᴇɴᴛʀᴀʟ ᴘʟᴀɪɴ of Ireland reaches the
Irish Sea between Dublin and Drogheda from which it
is separated by no more than low hills. The River Boyne,
famous in Irish history, rises in the Central Plain some 30 miles
west of Dublin, and flows north-west through Trim, Navan
and Slane to reach the sea. Through the greater part of its
course it flows through County Meath though it rises in West
Meath; these two counties, which originally formed the ancient
province of Meath, contain probably the most important sites
in the whole of Ireland's prehistory and ancient history. In its
course the Boyne passes some of these famous sites such as the
great early monastic site of Clonard, the fine medieval buildings
at Trim, the ruins of the Cistercian monastery at Bective, and
slightly to the south, the royal site of Tara; while on its northern
bank is the village and hill of Slane associated with Tara in the
story of the opening of St Patrick's mission. Beyond Slane is
the site of the Battle of the Boyne in which William of Orange
defeated the Stuart King James II in 1690 and won the crown
of England.

The main tributary of the Boyne—the Blackwater—flows   *Fig. 1*
through the town of Kells with its numerous remains of the
famous early Christian monastery, originally founded to house
the relics of St Columcille brought from Iona in the early
ninth century because of Viking raids on that west Scottish
island monastery. Immediately beyond Slane the Boyne forms
a semicircular loop to the south; this is the Bend of the Boyne
and here are the archaeological sites which form the subject of
this book. This loop is in County Meath just before the river
crosses the boundary into County Louth to reach the sea a

few miles further on in the town of Drogheda—a town which played a sad and important part in the Cromwellian campaigns in Ireland, and which still preserves interesting medieval build/ ings. The location of some of these places is shown on the map. A general description of this delightful and historically exciting part of Ireland was given by Sir William Wilde in his *The Beauties of the Boyne and its Tributary the Blackwater*. Wilde (1815–76) was a Dublin surgeon and antiquary, whose own fame has perhaps been eclipsed by that of his son, Oscar, the poet and dramatist. Sir William wrote on surgery, on archae/ ology and topography, and his book on the Boyne (first pub/ lished in 1849 with a second edition in 1850, and a third in 1949 in which his editor, Colm ÓLochlainn, rather extrava/ gantly describes him as 'the first, and still the greatest of our scientific archaeologists') was based on material collected, he tells us, 'during excursions made from time to time, to the Boyne, for health, amusement, or instruction'. Wilde's account is still a delightful piece of topographical writing as well as of value archaeologically for its description of the Boyne sites in the mid/nineteenth century.

Plates 1, 2, 37, 38, 50

Fig. 2

The loop in the river—the Bend of the Boyne—is about 5 miles across: here first are a series of small glacial hillocks rising out of the flood plain of the river, and on these have been con/ structed the three great prehistoric mounds or barrows known as New Grange, Dowth and Knowth of which New Grange and Dowth contain and cover great stone tombs; it is generally thought that Knowth also does so, although no tomb has as yet been located there. The names Dowth and Knowth are modern versions of old Irish Dubadh and Cnodhba, and it has been suggested that New Grange might be an English corruption of *An Uamh Greinè* (i.e. the cave of Grainnè, a mythological Irish figure who made a tour of Ireland in a year and a day and carried large stones in her apron that were some/ times thrown down to make her bed), which would have been

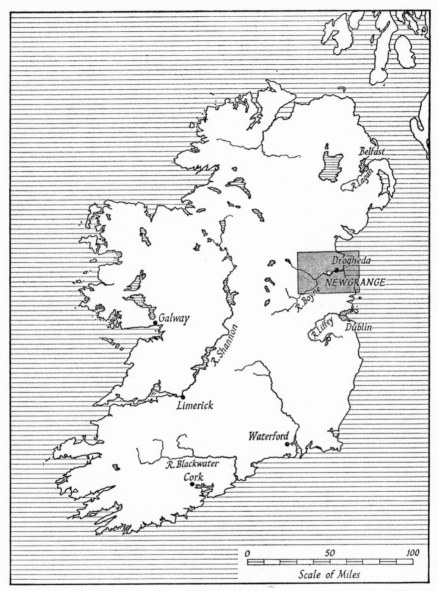

Fig. 1. The position of New Grange and the Bend of the Boyne sites in relation to Ireland. (Shaded area is Fig. 2)

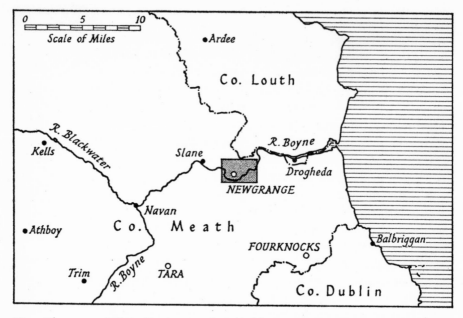

Fig. 2. The area occupied by prehistoric sites in the Bend of the Boyne. (Shaded area is Fig. 20)

pronounced something like *noovgrainy*, but it seems more likely that it is a straightforward Anglo-Irish estate name.

New Grange is the best known of these three monuments, but all three must rank among the most magnificent burial mounds of their type in Western Europe. Together with them is a series of other mounds and monuments, the whole forming a large prehistoric cemetery which shows very clearly the great importance of this area in prehistoric times for the builders of the great stone tombs usually referred to in archaeological literature as megaliths or chamber tombs. New Grange is cer-tainly one of the finest of these prehistoric megalithic chamber tombs in Europe and it would certainly have to be in any list of the seven or nine prehistoric wonders of Atlantic Europe, along with Stonehenge, the stone rows of Carnac in Brittany, and Maes Howe in the Orkneys. And it is as important and worthy of constant and detailed study, as it is impressive. In his Presidential Address to the Royal Irish Academy in 1927 the late R. A. S. Macalister, then Professor of Archaeology in University College, Dublin, said. 'If we could answer all the questions directly or indirectly raised by New Grange and the allied mounds, we might fairly claim to know everything that can be known about the Bronze Age in Ireland. Almost all roads in the study of this period of our country's history lead sooner or later to New Grange.'

It is natural that impressive monuments like New Grange and Stonehenge should be visited a great deal by the general public and should themselves have attracted a folklore based on imagination, half-forgotten history, unappreciated archaeology and the sort of nonsense that luxuriates in the lunatic fringes of serious archaeology. The visitor to New Grange and Dowth will not be surprised to be told that these monuments were built by and were the homes of 'the little people' or to be asked their connection with the Druids. A coloured calendar current in Ireland in 1960 had in it a good photograph of the decorated stone at the entrance to New Grange; this was accompanied by an account which needs quoting almost *in toto* as an example of the jumble of nonsense and wishful thinking indulged in by those who prefer the pleasures of the irrational and the joys of unreason to the hard thinking that archaeology demands. 'The entrance in the east was originally triangular,' says this description, 'but is now changed for easy entrance, formerly it was necessary to crawl in and progress was retarded by interference, stones compelling the neophyte to stoop and stumble. The rays of the rising sun at certain times of the year penetrate the opening and rest on a remarkable triple spiral carving in the central chamber. Like the Great Pyramid of Gizeh in Egypt the New Grange Temple was originally covered with a layer of white quartz and was a brilliant object of Light for a considerable distance. Nuda, first king of

Tuatha de Danann in Ireland, and his Master Magician, are said to have officiated here in the very, very old days. Artemi-doros the Ephesian stated: "To Sacred Ierne of the Hibernians men go to learn more of the Mysteries of Samothrace."'

It is at least true in this strange wild-cat account we have just quoted, that New Grange might well be described as belonging to 'the very, very old days'. It is our object in this book not only to describe the great tombs in the Bend of the Boyne but to set them in what appears to us their true prehistoric context, as far as the limitations of archaeology allow, eschewing the little people and Artemidoros. In this chapter it is proposed to describe New Grange itself as it appears today and as we know it through history, and therefore to try to assess what it looked like when first built and used. We shall leave until the next chapter a full account of the art on the stones of New Grange which make it one of the most exciting monuments of early north-western Europe. Chapter III will be concerned with Dowth and Knowth and the other prehistoric remains in the Bend of the Boyne. The fourth chapter will describe other monuments in Ireland and Britain which have affinities and connections with the Boyne tombs, and the final chapter will deal with the problems of the purpose and origins of these monuments. For those who are not acquainted with the cus-tomary terminology of great stone tombs and who cannot at once consult the various statements on this subject listed in the bibliography we must first preface our account of New Grange as it is today with a few words of explanation.

MEGALITHS AND CHAMBER TOMBS

The term megalith or megalithic monument is normally ap-plied to the great prehistoric stone monuments of north-western Europe, and there are four main kinds: the *menhir* or single standing stone, the alignment or stone row (of which the alignments in Brittany are the most famous), stone circles (of which Avebury and Stonehenge in Wessex are outstanding), and the tombs, or chamber tombs, like New Grange and Maes Howe. These stone tombs are usually constructed with walls of large upright stones called orthostats or with walls of unmortared or dry stone walling. Often a combination of both was used, as when the interstices between the edges of the orthostats are filled with intercalary dry walling or as when the orthostats are backed by dry walling, both being bonded together at the top to form what has become generally known as the 'classic megalithic wall'. The tombs are usually roofed with large horizontal megaliths called capstones, or with a false or cor-belled vault made of successive layers of oversailing stones. New Grange itself has one of the finest corbelled vaults surviving from antiquity. The phrase 'large' is advisedly used in describing most megalithic constructions; it is not uncommon to have orthostats 12 feet long by 8 feet high and capstones weighing 20 to 40 tons, and the phrase 'chamber tomb' means that the structures are rooms or chambers into which the average-sized man or woman can walk erect. It is a feature of megalithic architecture that the stones used, while for the most part tabular, are only roughly dressed, and do not normally have straight edges or plane surfaces. It is one of the great interests of New Grange, itself a *tour de force* in megalithic tomb architecture (as it is of Stonehenge, itself a *tour de force* in megalithic temple architecture), that there is a considerable amount of very careful dressing of the stones.

These chamber tombs are usually incorporated in a heap of earth or stones variously referred to as a tumulus or barrow or cairn, and the form which this barrow takes may be long, or round—as it is at New Grange, Dowth and Knowth. The edge of the barrow may be defined by a kerb or revetment wall of orthostats or dry walling, and sometimes there is a free-standing circle of stones around the barrow as there is at New

Grange. The entrance to the chamber is often defined by a forecourt which may vary in shape from cuspate to concave—the semicircular or concave forecourt is a common feature of some types of tombs.

Fig. 3

There is a wide variety of form among the many thousands of megalithic chamber tombs that survive from prehistoric times in Western Europe, but two very common and well-known forms are the Passage Grave and the Gallery Grave (or *allée couverte* in the French nomenclature). The Passage Grave consists of a passage leading into a central chamber, whereas the Gallery Grave, or *allée couverte*, consists of a long parallel-sided chamber. Sometimes tombs of either main type may be divided up by sill-stones, just a few inches high, or septal slabs up to half or more than half the height of the chamber. Septal slabs may be perforated to form port-hole entrances into a delimited section of a tomb.

There are in various parts of Western Europe many folk-names for chambered tombs and other megalithic monuments such as *Samson's Bratful* or *Dermot and Grainnè's Bed* (it has already been mentioned that the name Grainnè may be involved in New Grange) or *The Devil's Quoit*; and there are also general folk-names of a generic kind. Thus in Sardinia groups of tombs are referred to as Giants' Graves. In Wales the word *cromlech* is used as a general designation for megalithic tombs, but it should be remembered that in France this means a stone circle. In France the general name for a chamber tomb is *dolmen*, but this word has been given a wide variety of special connotations by scholars, notably its use to mean the *dysse/dös* tombs of Scandinavia. It seems best not to use the term *dolmen* in any specialized way, but of course it can be used in the general French sense, and it was in this sense that W. C. Borlase used it in his three-volume work *The Dolmens of Ireland* published in 1897. In Ireland and western Britain the term *portal-dolmen* is used to describe a monument consisting of a single rectilinear

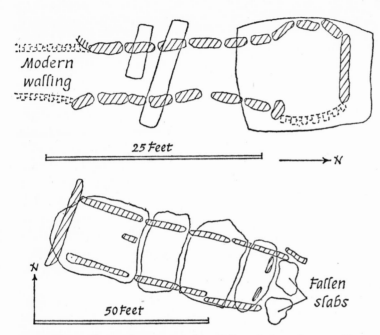

Modern
walling

25 Feet

N

50 Feet

Fallen
slabs

Fig. 3. Plans to illustrate the main types of megalithic tombs in north-western Europe: (top) a Passage Grave; (bottom) a Gallery Grave

chamber usually narrowing towards the back with an entry be-tween two tall portal stones, and this is a useful term, although we prefer to use the phrase *portal-chamber*. Indeed wherever the term *dolmen* is specifically qualified in any way it can produce a valuable term.

In the East Mediterranean the term *tholos* is used for a circular tomb approached by a passage or *dromos*, such as the Treasury of Atreus at Mycenae; and this term has been used by many writers to describe the corbel-vaulted tombs of Western Europe. Thus New Grange is often described as a *tholos*, so is Maes Howe, and so are Ile Longue and the tombs in the south Iberian cemeteries of Alcalá and Los Millares. It would seem

most convenient to restrict the term *tholos* to the East Mediterranean tombs. This does not, of course, mean that the East
Mediterranean *tholoi* and the tombs just referred to from Atlantic
Europe may not be generically connected. Indeed this is one
of the important issues that will be discussed in our final chapter. If the word *tholos* is used in Western Europe we shall find
ourselves calling New Grange a *tholos* and Ile Longue in
Brittany a *tholos* whereas the fine Passage Grave of Gavrinis in
Brittany which is orthostatically walled and roofed by megalithic capstones would not be so called: and yet the art on the
walls of Gavrinis is closely paralleled by the art at New Grange.
It would not be convenient or prudent to draw a formal and
nomenclatural line between tombs which are functionally and
formally alike and decorated in the same way.

There are many variants of the basic plans of Passage Graves
and Gallery Graves, and we shall have to mention some of
these later in this book. One variety occurs when side chambers
are added to the basic tomb plan; when pairs of side chambers
occur in Gallery Graves they are referred to as Transepted
Gallery Graves, and the fine Cotswold monuments like Hetty
Pegler's Tump and Notgrove and the Wessex tomb of West
Kennet, are good examples of this type. Passage Graves may
have one, two or three side chambers, and a particularly Irish
arrangement is that in which three side chambers open out of
the main chamber to give a cruciform plan. New Grange is a
cruciform Passage Grave. Another variant of the Passage Grave
occurs in which the demarcation between passage and chamber
is not clearly shown: the resultant form is a sort of wedge or V
in plan. Some of these wedge-shaped or V-shaped Passage
Graves occur in Ireland, as in south-west Britain and Brittany
and the Channel Islands; they are often referred to as Undifferentiated Passage Graves, and when small and almost parallel-
sided, as Entrance Graves. There are also wedge-shaped Gallery Graves and reference will have to be made briefly to these

in discussing the interrelations of the various Irish groups of megalithic monuments.

Megalithic tombs are only one constructional variant of prehistoric tombs used collectively by family or neighbourhood groups as burial vaults perhaps over a long period of time. Another constructional variant is the rock-cut tomb, but no convincing examples of this type have been found in the British Isles or north-western France. Rock-cut tombs exist, however, in southern Portugal and Spain, in the Champagne area of northern France, in southern France, Sardinia, the Balearics, Malta and Sicily, for example, and it will be necessary to consider these tombs when discussing the affinities and origins of the Irish Passage Graves and their art.

This is necessarily only a very brief summary of the main aspects of megalithic terminology, and, as we have said at the beginning, for a detailed treatment of this topic readers are advised to consult the books mentioned in the bibliography. For those who come fresh to the study of prehistoric megaliths it should be said here that the generally accepted view is that the floruit of megalithic tomb construction is between the first quarter of the third millennium and the first quarter of the second millennium B.C., i.e. a bracket of 3000 to 1750 B.C. would be a conservative estimate; but there is evidence accumulating, as we write, from Brittany to suggest that there the earliest chamber tombs were built between 3500 and 3000 B.C., whereas some tombs were being used (and some built) as late as 1000 B.C. We will also see that some have argued in special cases—Dr Joseph Raftery on re-excavating Loughcrew H, for example—that megalithic tomb construction went on into the Early Iron Age, that is to say as late as the first or second century A.D. But all these matters of chronology will be discussed later. Let us now leave the aridities of nomenclature, classification and chronology, and take a look at New Grange itself.

NEW GRANGE TODAY

Plates 1, 2

What do we see at the present day when we get to the Bend of the Boyne and look at New Grange? A round barrow just over 40 feet high and 280 feet in diameter covering about an

Plate 3

acre of ground. The mound has, set up around it, and free from it, twelve large stones forming part of a surrounding freestanding stone circle. In front of the entrance to the chamber is

Figs. 4, 5

a large decorated stone—one of the two most famous stones at New Grange, and indeed one of the most famous stones in the whole repertory of European megalithic art; this stone is part of a kerb circle and two other megaliths of this kerb are visible; they are marked *a* and *b* on the plan, the decorated kerb-stone

Plate 6

at the entrance is Coffey's *c*. Connecting these megalithic kerb-stones is a stone wall surrounding and retaining the mound —this is a modern feature as is the ditch in front of this wall and the bank on the outside of the ditch, although this bank may

Plate 4

contain some original spill from the barrow itself. The barrow, as we see it today, is partly surfaced with stones including quartz pebbles but is mainly grass-covered.

In the south-east quadrant of the mound and leading in from the decorated kerb-stone *c* is a passage 62 feet in length leading into a central chamber from 8 to 10 feet across from which open out three side chambers. Although these strictly speaking face south-west, north-west and north-east, they may, for convenience of reference, be described as the south, west and north side chambers or left, end and right side chambers, just as the stones of the passage are usually referred to as left or right, starting from the entrance. The passage and the chambers are walled with big stone slabs or orthostats; there are twenty-two orthostats along the left-hand side of the passage and twenty-one along the right-hand side, whilst the walls of the cruciform chamber contain seventeen. These with their

Fig. 6

reference numbers are shown on the plan.

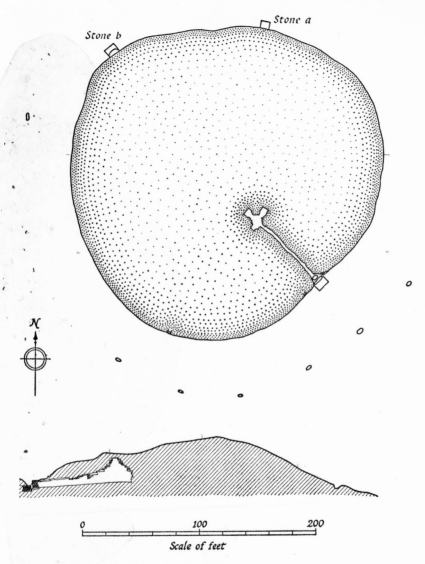

Figs. 4, 5. Plan of the mound of New Grange (Fig. 4).
South-North section through the mound of New Grange (Fig. 5).

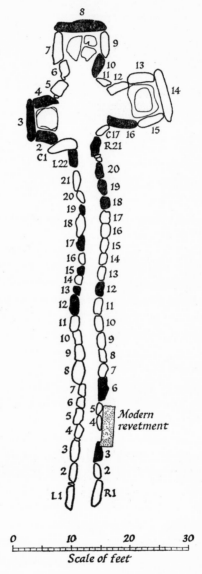

Fig. 6. Plan of chamber at New Grange based on Coffey. The decorated stones are marked in black, and all are numbered according to Coffey's list

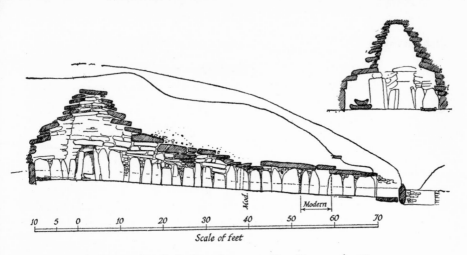

Fig. 7. Longitudinal section through chamber and passage at New Grange, and section at right-angles through chamber and side chambers

The orthostats of the passage are from 5 to 8 feet in height, and vary in length up to 12 feet. The width of the passage is about 3 feet, but at about 14 feet from the entrance the side stones meet at the top giving a triangular section and making it necessary to crawl on hands and knees for about 6 feet. At the entrance the passage is just under 5 feet high; it then rises to 6 feet for a distance of 26 feet, drops to under 5 feet again, rises to 7 feet 10 inches at 43 feet from the entrance, falls again to 4 feet 10 inches, and finally rises once more as it merges into the roof of the chamber. This variation in roof level is shown in the section. The passage is roofed with large capstones, one of them as long as 15 feet, resting directly on the heads of the orthostats or rather on the classic megalithic wall of orthostats and dry walling.

Plates 7–9

The chamber is roofed with a fine corbel vault springing from the dry walling, and with large horizontal stones behind the vertical orthostats of the chamber. The chamber is 19 feet 6 inches high; the over-all dimensions are, from the end of the passage to the back of the west side chamber 18 feet, and from the south of the south recess to the north of the north recess

Fig. 7
Plate 10

21 feet. The three side chambers are in part roofed by capstones, but these also serve as corbels in the construction of the corbel vault over the main central chamber. The central chamber itself is roughly 10 feet across.

Plates 11, 12

The south side chamber has on the floor a large stone basin about 3 feet 6 inches across and the western side chamber has a broken stone basin 3 feet 6 inches across by 6 feet long. There are two stone basins in the northern side chamber, the lower, flatter one being 6 feet across, the upper one 3 feet 6 inches by 4 feet, carefully made and with a design of two hollows on its western edge. This carefully wrought upper basin was to be found for a while in the middle of the central chamber, and was there in Coffey's descriptions of fifty years ago, but it seems that it was placed there in error by those demanding the symmetry of a basin in every chamber; it is now back in the north side chamber where it seems to have been originally.

This brief account gives a picture of New Grange as it is today. Before we can try to picture what it was like originally, we must study the accounts of this monument given by anti-quaries in the eighteenth and nineteenth centuries.

NEW GRANGE IN HISTORY

It has been said that New Grange is the most well known of the prehistoric sites in the Bend of the Boyne, and it was naturally New Grange which attracted the earliest travellers who have left accounts of their antiquarian travels in Ireland. The first of these was the Welsh antiquary Edward Lhwyd (1660–1708), a man who was described by Sir John Rhŷs as 'in many respects the greatest Celtic philologist the world has ever seen', but who was also, with his contemporary John Aubrey, in many ways the founder of modern field archaeology. Lhwyd was a polymath in the true seventeenth-century use of that term; he travelled widely in Celtic countries observing the manners and customs of the people, their language, their anti/ quities, and the natural world in which they lived. He crossed to Ireland at the end of August or the beginning of September 1699 and in Dublin was welcomed by members of the Philo/ sophical Society. He travelled through Ireland to Scotland, and was back again in Ireland at the end of February 1700; he now journeyed westward and was back in Wales in April.

In two letters we have Lhwyd's accounts of his impressions of New Grange. They are interesting not only because they tell us a great deal about this very important Irish monument two hundred and fifty years ago, but because they constitute one of the very earliest accounts of a megalithic tomb in anti/ quarian literature, and should be set alongside the accounts of the excavations of a typical Paris Basin Gallery Grave at Cocherel near Dreux in the valley of the Eure. Olivier Estienne's remarkable account of this Cocherel excavation was in a document dated 11 July 1685, though it was not published until Le Brasseur wrote his *Histoire Civile et Ecclésiastique du Comté d'Evreux* in 1722—this book also contains an interesting note by the Abbé of Cocherel on the tomb. Estienne, the Abbé of Cocherel, and Montfaucon in his *L'Antiquité expliquée et représéntée en figures* (1719, with David Humphrey's English translation in 1722), were much concerned in speculating about the Cocherel tomb: Who built it? When? Why? Edward Lhwyd had the very same questions to ask of himself and others as he wrote about New Grange.

Lhwyd's first letter was written at Bathgate near Linlithgow to Dr Tancred Robinson on 15 December 1699. He said, 'The most remarkable curiosity we saw by the way was a stately Mount at a place called New Grange near Drogheda; having a number of huge stones pitch'd on end round about it, and a single one on the top. The gentleman of the village (one Mr Charles Campbel) observing that under the green turf this mount was wholly composed of stones, and having occasion for some, employ'd his servants to carry off a considerable parcel of them; till they came at last to a very broad flat stone, rudely carved, and placed edgewise at the bottom of the mount. This they discovered to be the door of a cave, which had a long entry leading to it. At the first entering we were forced to creep; but still as we went on, the pillars on each side of us were higher and higher; and coming into the cave we found it about 20 foot high. In this cave, on each hand of us was a cell or apartment, and another went straight forward opposite to the entry. In those on each hand was a very broad shallow bason of stone, situated at the edge. The bason in the right hand apartment stood in another; that on the left was single, and in the apartment straight forward there was none at all. We observed that water dropt into the right hand bason, tho' it had rained but little in many days; and suspected that the lower bason was intended to preserve the superfluous liquor of the upper (whether this water was sacred, or whether it was for Blood in Sacrifice) that none might come to the ground. The great pillars round this cave, supporting the mount, were not at all hewn or wrought; but were such rude stones as those of Abury in Wiltshire, and rather more rude than those of Stonehenge; but those about the basons, and some else-where, had such barbarous sculpture (viz. spiral like a snake, but without distinction of head and tail) as the forementioned stone at the entry of the cave. There was no flagging nor floor to this entry nor cave, but any sort of loose stones every where under feet. They found several bones in the cave and part of a Stags (or else Elks) head, and some other things, which I omit, because the labourers differ'd in their account of them. A gold coin of the Emperor Valentinian, being found near the top of this mount, might bespeak it Roman; but that the rude carving at the entry and in the cave seems to denote it a bar-barous monument. So, the coin proving it ancienter than any Invasion of the Ostmans or Danes, and the carving and rude sculpture, barbarous; it should follow, that it was some place of sacrifice or burial of the ancient Irish.'

The second letter of Lhwyd's was sent from Sligo in March 1700 to the Reverend Henry Rowlands, Vicar of Llanrhidian in Anglesey. Rowlands was himself a keen archaeologist and author of *Mona Antiqua Restaurata*, published in 1723, in which he 'restores' Anglesey to the Druids. This letter adds some fresh observations to those in the letter to Tancred Robin, son. 'I also met with one monument in this kingdom very singular,' wrote Lhwyd. 'It stands at a place called New Grange . . . and is a Mount or Barrow of very considerable height encompass'd with vast stones pitch'd on end round the bottom of it; *and having another lesser standing on the top*. The Mount is all the work of hands, and consists almost wholly of stones, but is cover'd with gravel and greenswerd, and has within it a remarkable cave . . . the entry was guarded all along on each side with such rude stones pitch'd on end, some of them having the same carving, and *other vast ones laid a-cross these at top*. The out pillars were so close pressed by the weight of the Mount that they admitted but just creeping in . . . under feet there was nothing but loose stones of any size in confusion; and amongst them a great many bones of beasts and some pieces of deers horns.' Then Lhwyd repeats to Rowlands his earlier observation about the date of the tomb: 'Near the top of this Mount they found a gold coin of the Emperor Valentinian, but, notwithstanding this, the rude carving above-mentioned makes me conclude this monument was never Roman not to mention that we want history to prove that ever the Romans were at all in Ireland.'

These letters of Lhwyd's seem to preserve an account of the first discovery of the burial chamber at New Grange, late in the seventeenth century, and also valuable information, to which reference will be made later, about the state of the monument at that time, the finds in the chamber, the position of the 'basons', and the presence of a standing stone on the top of the mound. It is interesting to note that while the Abbé of Cocherel was deciding that the Cocherel megalithic tomb was filled with the bodies of Huns arrived in France under Attila, and Montfaucon that it belonged to 'some barbarous Nation that knew not yet the Use of either Iron or of any metal', Lhwyd was firmly setting New Grange in its proper place as a monument of the pre-Roman Irish.

The next account of New Grange that is relevant to the present purpose is by Thomas Molyneux, Professor of Physick in the University of Dublin, also, as described on the title page of his book, 'Physician to the State, and Physician General to the Army in Ireland'. Molyneux wrote *A Discourse concerning the Danish Mounts, Forts and Towers in Ireland* which was pub-lished in 1725 as the third part of *A Natural History of Ireland in Three Parts, by several hands,* and published in Dublin by George Grierson 'at the Two Bibles in Essex Street'. Molyneux was very critical of Irish writers before his time who 'deduce their stock from generations near the flood . . . invent ante-diluvian stories, and a fable of a niece of *Noah* himself landing in this island.' He argued that the oldest inhabitants of Ireland were from Great Britain and were 'Celtick Gauls', and that the oldest human monuments in Ireland were not products of these people but of the Danes, 'foreigners, a strange nation that invaded and settled in this island some time between the eighth and ninth century after Christ'. New Grange was, then, to Molyneux, a *Danes-Mount,* and 'raised in honour of some mighty prince, or person of the greatest power and dignity of his time'. Molyneux had visited the site and describes how remarkable it seemed to him: he makes it, however, 1000 feet in circumference, 150 feet high, and measured it 300 feet round the flat surface at the top. He notes the stones around the foot of the barrow, some of which he said were 11, others not 4 feet high, and he says that the entrance 'was but lately discovered . . . by accident in removing part of the stones to make a pavement in the neighbourhood. The bottom of the cave and entry is a rude sort of pavement, made of the same stones of which the mount is composed, not beaten or joined together, but loosely cast upon the ground only to cover it. Along the middle of the cave a slender quarry-stone, five or six foot long, lies on the floor, shaped like a pyramid, that once, as I imagine, stood upright, perhaps a central stone to those placed round the outside of the mount: but now 'tis fallen down. . . . When first the cave was opened, the bones of two dead bodies entire, not burnt, were found upon the floor, in likelyhood the reliques of a husband and his wife, whose conjugal affection had joyn'd them in their grave as in their bed.'

Molyneux then goes on to say that in each of the three cells, i.e. in each of the three side chambers off the main chamber, was 'a broad and shallow cistern, somewhat round, but rudely formed out of a kind of free-stone', and that the cistern in the right-hand or northern side chamber was 'better shaped and in the middle of it was placed another smaller cistern, better wrought and of a more curious make.' He describes the occurrence of decorated stones, decorated, he says, with a 'barbarous kind of carving', but nowhere was he able to find 'the least footsteps of writing', which convinced him that the Danes in Ireland were illiterate. The cisterns or basins, he thought, were 'certainly designed for altars, to offer sacrifice upon to pagan Gods, in favour of the dead; and being three in number, shew they were dedicated to the deities of the three prime idols, religiously adored by all the nations of the north.' He published a plan by a Mr Samuel Molyneux, 'a young gentleman of the college of Dublin'. This plan shows the general layout of the monument correctly, with the 'cisterns' in each side chamber and the fallen stone in the centre of the central chamber, and also two Roman gold coins, one of Valentinian and one of Theodosius, which were found, he says, 'removing about ten

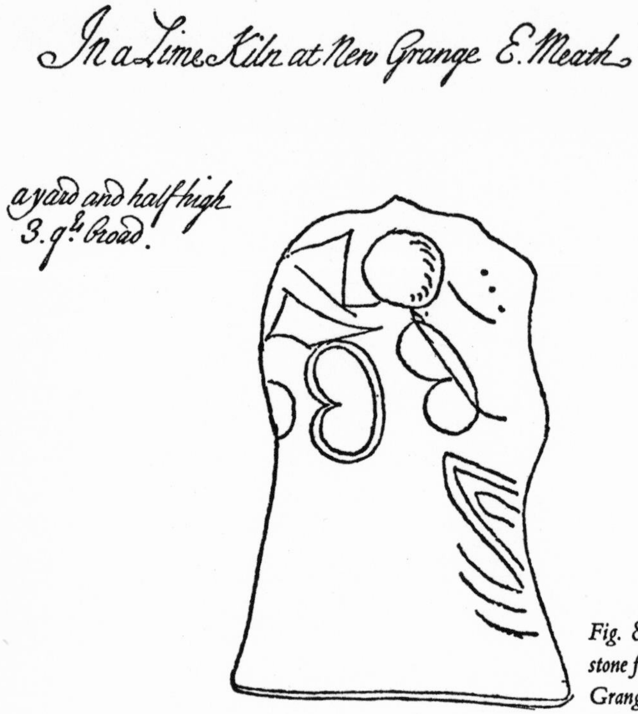

In a Lime Kiln at New Grange E. Meath

a yard and half high
3. q.ᵗ broad.

Fig. 8. Drawing by Anstis of a stone found in a lime kiln near New Grange. (B.M. Stowe MS. 1024)

or twelve years since some of the heap of stones on the outside of the mount'.

Molyneux also drew attention to Knowth and Dowth, 'these two *tumuli* being of a smaller size,' he wrote, 'seem prob- ably raised as sepulchres for the children, or kindred of those persons that lie buried under the greatest mount,' and goes on in a charming way to speculate about the name New Grange 'as of the three mounts altogether were designed by way of a family monument for some great Danish prince, that chose to be interred near his country-dwelling, that might be hereabouts, as the word *Grange* seems to imply,' and he then goes on to quote from Olaus Wormius, whose authority he much re- spected, that the Danes often chose their burying places near their country seats.

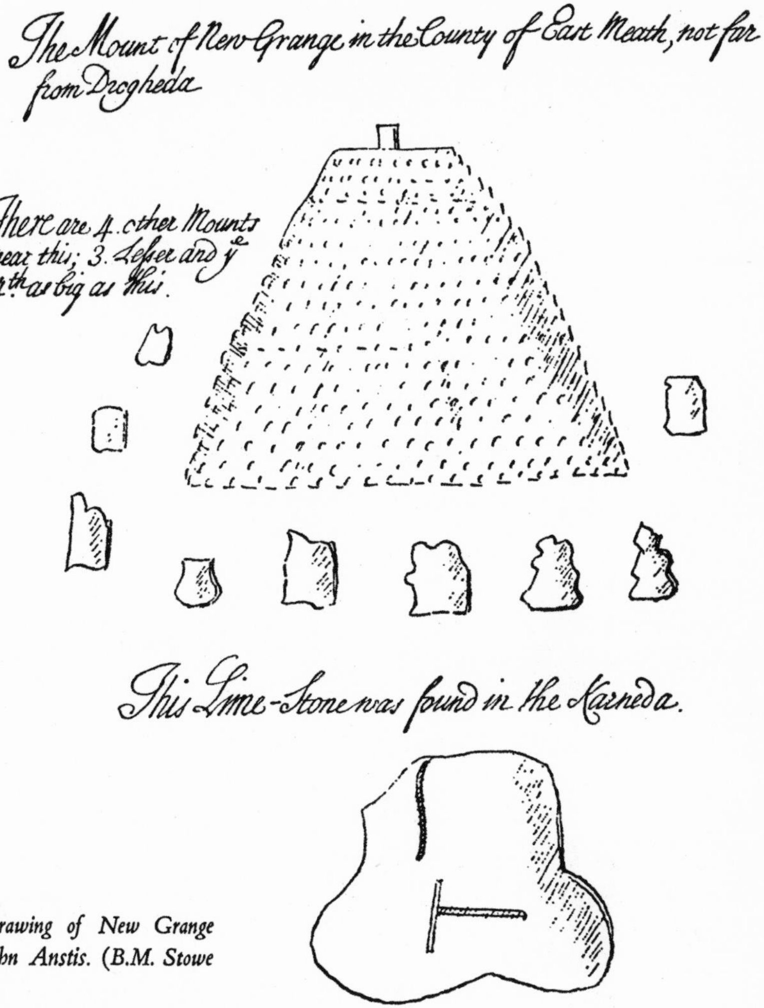

The Mount of New Grange, in the County of East Meath, not far from Drogheda

There are 4 other Mounts near this; 3. lesser and ye 4th as big as this.

This Lime-Stone was found in the Karneda.

Fig. 9. Drawing of New Grange made by John Anstis. (B.M. Stowe MS. 1024)

John Anstis (1669–1745) was a junior contemporary of Edward Lhwyd and travelled extensively in the British Isles recording ancient monuments. He visited New Grange and in his manuscript account (now in the British Museum: BM Stowe 1024) he has a drawing of New Grange, reproduced *Figs. 8, 9* here, showing clearly the stone on top of the mound, and one of another stone 'found in a lime kiln at New Grange', which is decorated in the style of megalithic art.

Molyneux and Anstis and Lhwyd were writing at a time when a purely archaeological approach to the problems of pre/history was not possible; the most that could be done was to describe the ancient remains in terms of known ancient peoples —the Celts, the Romans, the Greeks, the Phoenicians, the Egyptians. This is of course not to decry the work of anti/quaries at the time—they worked according to their lights, but sometimes the lights were very strange and we pass over into the lunatic fringes of the subject previously referred to. One such who dwelt there was Colonel Charles Vallancey whose *Vindication of the Ancient History of Ireland* was published in 1786: New Grange to Vallancey was a Mithraic temple— Grange itself meant 'den of Grian' or 'Mithras'. He compares it with the one he alleged had been found in Wales in 1778 and says, 'These are the works of the old Scotti, prior to the arrival of the Cymmerigh in Britain.' He comments on the engraving

Plate 25

which is now generally referred to as Coffey's ship and finds that it is an inscription in Ogham, reading it as '*Angus*, the name of an Arch/Druid, or more likely *Angbein*, the Holy Ones'. Poor Colonel Vallancey—yet he had one merit: he called forth the wonderful parody published in 1790 under the title of *Eymetomena or the Antiquities of Killmackumpshaugh*, and for that we must be ever grateful.

Forty/five years after Molyneux's book was on sale in Dublin, Governor Pownall visited New Grange and wrote a long account of it in a letter to the Reverend Dr Sharpe, Master of the Temple. This letter was read at a meeting of the Society of Antiquaries of London—indeed it was such a long letter that it seems to have been read at two meetings, namely those of 21 and 28 June 1770. It was published in Volume II of *Archaeologia* in 1773. Pownall's account is in itself very in/

teresting and a characteristic piece of archaeological writing of the eighteenth century. 'Accident', he says, 'about the end of the last century discovered an opening in the side of the great Pyramid at New Grange in Ireland.' It was, he thought, 'a superb and eminently magnificent monument . . . though now but a ruinous frustrum of what it once was . . . a pyramid of stone, compiled of pebble or cogle stones, such as are commonly used in paving.' Pownall studied the monument with great care, 'examining very narrowly, with a candle in my hand, all the parts of this cemetery,'—indeed he seems to have stayed there too long, for he says, 'as I had continued in this cave a much longer time than was prudent, by which I caught a violent illness.' Pownall had nothing good to say about the accounts of Lhwyd and Molyneux: Lhwyd's account was 'conceived in too general terms', and as for Molyneux, 'the measurements are not exact; his observations upon particular parts are hasty, inattentive and not just; and the drawings are mere deformities, made out at random.' Poor Dr Molyneux! He had made New Grange 150 feet high; Pownall got a Mr Samuel Bovie to make more detailed measurements and prepare a plan, and Bovie made it 42 feet high which is approximately correct. But Pownall rejected the figures of his own surveyor while admitting that he approached 'nearest the truth'; he himself made the barrow 70 feet in height. He described ten kerb-stones of which nine were erect and one recumbent. He could find no trace of the stone which Lhwyd saw on the top of the barrow.

Pownall drew particular attention to the stone in the southern side chamber (C 4) with the curious engraved pattern which Coffey and others have thought to be a stylized ship-motif, and which Colonel Vallancey read as an Ogham inscription. Pownall was himself sure it was writing and that the 'characters are evidently neither Irish, Runic nor Saxon. . . . I have persuaded myself', he goes on, 'that this inscription is

Phoenician, and contains only numerals.' He thought it was part of an ancient monument re-used at New Grange, and that it had originally been part of 'a marine or naval monument erected at the mouth of the Boyne by some of these Eastern people to whom the ports of Ireland were well known.' This monu-ment, he considered, fell into ruin and parts of it were re-used in building the barrow of New Grange. Pownall had no doubt that it was made by the Danes and was an example of the monuments found also in Sweden, Russia, Poland, and com-pares it with the 'Bougres in the Steppe of Tartary, but is also sensible of similar monuments in the Balearics and presses comparisons with the Pyramids of Egypt.'

At the end of his account Pownall is prompted to write a splendid romantic passage which we cannot forbear to quote; it does, anyway, in fine eighteenth-century style summarize the reflections which any person of sensibility must have at New Grange. 'When one considers the multitude of hands, the length of time, the boundless expence, which conspired to form this stupendous monument,' he wrote, 'when one reflects on the transparent spirit of ambition which formed the idea of this great and simple magnificence, dedicated to the memory of some great person; one cannot but repine at the caprice of fate and fame, that while one sees the magnificence, one finds that the name, which it was to perpetuate, is gone. Such is glory, when it is past; such is fame. One sees the traces of something great and active having passed by; but the thing itself is gone . . . Its glory was a momentary vision; and the fame of it, like the baseless fabrick of that vision, is dissolved.'

Edward Ledwich in his *Antiquities of Ireland* (1790, second edition 1803) republishes Pownall's plan and section but adds little to our knowledge of the site. He thought that the 'boat-like figure of our urns', by which he means the stone basins, indicated to him that 'the persons for whom they were de-signed' were 'naval commanders. A ship was their most be-

loved object in life, and their sepulchres were of this shape.'
Ledwich disapproved of Lhwyd's idea of dating the monument from the two coins, and says firmly that it was built in
the ninth century A.D. and was part of the Norse raids on
eastern Ireland: 'A principal commander, dying at New
Grange, might have been interred there,' he says.

Three years after the first publication of Ledwich's *Antiquities of Ireland*, Sir Richard Colt Hoare, his plan to travel in the
Mediterranean and look at classical antiquities thwarted because these regions 'are interdicted to us by the ferocious de-
crees of a CORSICAN DESPOT', as he characteristically put it,
made an archaeological trip through Ireland which was published in 1807 as *Journal of a Tour in Ireland A.D. 1806*. He
visited New Grange, and compared it with the earthen tumuli
of the Wessex he knew, but it differed from the generality of
these, he said, 'by containing under its verdant surface, a subterraneous temple, constituted of the rudest materials and certainly of the highest antiquity.' He was much impressed by
the monument and described it in his general remarks (in
which he said he felt sure that a stone temple existed in ancient
times on the Curragh of Kildare) as 'one of the most curious
monuments of antiquity remaining within the limits of the
United Kingdom', and included a view of this 'subterraneous
temple' as his frontispiece. Colt Hoare seems to have been the
first to notice, or at least to describe in detail, the cup-shaped
depressions on the basin in the north side chamber. He did not
agree with the earlier writers who had made out some of the
engravings to be writing—Phoenician or Ogham—but compared the engraved patterns with those he had found on urns
in Wiltshire and was inclined 'to attribute this singular temple
to some of the Celtic or Belgic tribes who poured in upon us
from the Continent of Gaul.'

Mention has already been made of the two gold coins, one
of Valentinian and the other of Theodosius, both from the

Trier mint, which had been found at New Grange when Lhwyd was writing. In 1842 Lord Albert Conyngham wrote to Sir Henry Ellis, Secretary of the Society of Antiquaries of London, describing the finding of five gold ornaments at New Grange 'accidentally found by a labouring man about a fort, night since, within a few yards of the entrance to the caves at New Grange. They were at the depth of two feet from the surface of the ground, and without any covering or protection from the earth about them. Another labouring man, hearing of this discovery, carefully searched the spot whence they were taken, and found a *denarius* of Geta, and two other remains of small brass, but quite defaced.' This letter is in *Archaeologia* for 1844 (Volume 30, p. 137) together with a drawing show, ing the five objects, namely two finger-rings, two torque brace, lets, and a chain with hooks at the end. James Fergusson in his *Rude Stone Monuments in all Countries* (1872) says that at the same time 'a similar gold ring was found . . . in the cell,' gave the name of the possessor—a Mrs Caldwell—and made much of this ring because of what he thought was its evidence for dating New Grange. Mrs Celia Topp has studied the finds described by Lord Conyngham in her paper 'The Gold Ornaments Reputedly Found near the Entrance to New Grange in 1842', published in the Twelfth *Annual Report* of the Uni, versity of London Institute of Archaeology, and deduced that while the gold ring belonging to Mrs Caldwell might be dis, counted, the five gold objects formed a comparatively homo, geneous find, the chain belonging to the second or third, the bracelets to the third, and the rings to the fourth or fifth century A.D., and suggested it might all represent 'a votive offer, ing to a still-venerated deity outside his yet-hallowed sanctuary.'

George Wilkinson's *Practical Geology and Ancient Architecture of Ireland* (1845) discusses New Grange; he insists that the chamber was built of surface and not quarried rocks, and describes what may have been a closing stone, or *pierre de fermeture*, of the chamber: 'a large flat stone appears, from the peculiarity of its position, to have closed the entrance.' During these mid-century years, Sir William Wilde often visited New Grange and the other monuments in the Bend of the Boyne, and in his *The Beauties of the Boyne and its Tributary the Blackwater* (1849), a book dedicated to George Petrie (who had himself published an account of New Grange in *The Dublin Penny Journal* for 1833), he devotes the whole of Chapter VII to the Boyne tombs which were to him 'the Irish Memphis, or city of tombs'. He found seventeen sepulchral mounds and recorded his calculations that New Grange weighed 180,000 tons, covered two acres and was 80 feet high. He repeated comparisons he had heard between New Grange and Mycenaean architecture, was interested in the engravings, decided they were sacred carvings and coined the splendid word *Tymbo-glyphics* or tomb-writing for them; but he added 'that the meaning of these scriptures, if any such they have beyond being sacred to the dead, shall ever be brought to light from the haze of obscurity which now enshrouds them, is very problematical.'

When the Danish archaeologist J. J. A. Worsaae spent the winter of 1846–7 in Dublin during his nine months' visit to the British Isles, Patrick Chalmers wrote telling him that in Ireland at that time the usual interpretation was that both New Grange and Dowth were monuments of the Danes.

It was Wilde who first identified the Boyne barrows as the royal cemetery of Brugh na Boinne. He refers to the ancient account of the cemeteries known as 'Senchas na Relec', which is found in *Leabhar na h-Uidhre* (the *Book of the Dun Cow*) in the Royal Irish Academy, and he mentions the cemeteries which are enumerated there and excerpts the account of Brugh na Boinne, and then lists the monuments which are said to have existed there. Wilde states unhesitatingly that 'Brugh na Boinne was no other than the assemblage of mounds, caves, pillar-stones, and other sepulchral monuments, forming the great necropolis which extends along the left or northern bank of the river, from Slane to Netterville.' Speculation on this subject had already begun in the time of the Ordnance Survey when the great Irish scholar and antiquary John O'Donovan was working, under the aegis of the Survey, on the place names, legends and antiquities of the country. O'Donovan was every-where particularly anxious to locate the sites which are men-tioned in ancient descriptions and he, in several of the Ordnance letters—letters which he wrote from the field to his superiors in Dublin—speculated on the position of Brugh na Boinne. His speculation is mainly based on the story of Cormac Mac Airt, the King of Tara, who had, according to the tale, become Christian and asked to be buried not at the Boyne but at *Rath na Riogh*. O'Donovan gave reasons for believing that Brugh na Boinne is now Broad Boyne near Stackallen and repeats this assertion in his edition of the *Annals of the Four Masters*. O'Donovan was mainly concerned with countering a sugges-tion by Archdall, in the latter's manuscript work 'Hibernaiae Antiqua et Nova Nomenclature', that Brugh na Boinne was situated in the position now occupied by the town of Trim. In his anxiety over this issue and to establish the identity of Brugh na Boinne with Broad Boyne, O'Donovan states that the House of Cletty where Cormac lived was a fort in this area and that 'now let anyone skilled in the character and form of the pagan tombs of antiquity view the mounds at the place called Broadboyne by those who speak English and Brugh na Boinne by the Irish in the western part of the country, and he cannot avoid the conclusion that the tumuli congregated there are the tombs of the pagan monarchy of Ireland.'

In fact, however, there are no tombs on the south side of the river in the neighbourhood of the Broadboyne Bridge. The only antiquities to be seen there are a few scattered earthworks. And how much authority had O'Donovan for saying that the place was known as Brugh na Boinne by Irish-speakers?

George Petrie, an antiquary who wrote a famous work on the round towers of Ireland, in it quotes from the Senchas na Relec the description of Brugh na Boinne and also from Dindsenchas, another text found in various manuscripts which describe ancient Irish sites; but Petrie, although he mentions the mounds near the Boyne at Drogheda, Dowth and New Grange, does not specifically identify the site of Brugh na Boinne.

Sir William Wilde's identification is supported by the Reverend James O'Lavery in a note published in the *Journal of the Royal Society of Antiquaries of Ireland* in 1892, in which he cites names which incorporate the word Bro or Bru in the New Grange neighbourhood; but the manner in which he collected the names from the local people detracts somewhat from their value as evidence. However, this identification is unquestionably accepted by George Coffey, when he states in 1892 that the cemetery of tombs in the Bend of the Boyne 'has been identified as Brugh na Boinne.'

This problem of the identification of the Brugh na Boinne with the Boyne tombs arose here as an aside from a considera⁄ tion of the view of Sir William Wilde, who first put forward the idea in the first edition of his book in 1849. There is no need for us to chronicle the views and descriptions of New Grange that were published between Wilde and Coffey except to mention that Wakeman in his *Archaeologia Hibernica* (1811) published some good illustrations of the site and to note that all possible explanations of the monument and its art had by no means been exhausted by the late nineteenth century. The Reverend H. Estridge, for example, writing in the *Proceedings of the Oxford Architectural and Historical Society* for 1865 illus⁄ trates New Grange and its art—the illustrations, as W. C. Borlase says, charitably, 'surely drawn from memory', in which the art is made to look like medieval or even modern heraldry. It is obvious that great monuments attract all archaeologists to them, of all competences and prejudices.

In the late nineteenth century the first attempt at any excavation at New Grange took place. The Board of Works dug
round the edge of the mound, discovering the kerb circle of
stones and noting that many of them were decorated in the
same way as the stones in the chamber. It was this digging that
caused the bank and ditch effect which surrounds the monument and is not original. These late nineteenth-century excavations were filled in, only three of the decorated kerb-stones being
left visible, and a wall built to revet and face the mound. This
wall, the apparent ditch and the bank outside must be dis-
counted by present-day visitors.

We have at last arrived at the man who did most to describe
New Grange objectively and to study it in its widest European
contexts, namely George Coffey (1857–1916). Coffey was for
long Keeper of Irish Antiquities in the National Museum, and
was one of the great pioneer scholars of Irish archaeology. He
was also a modest man and was able to change his views with
regard to the historical and sociological context of New Grange
(as of other subjects he studied) in a completely radical way.
He began his detailed study of New Grange in 1890 and published several papers on this fascinating subject in the *Transac-
tions* and the *Proceedings* of the Royal Irish Academy, and the
Journal of the Royal Society of Antiquaries of Ireland. W. C. Borlase, in his *The Dolmens of Ireland*, a three-volume work published in 1897 (and a work of far greater value than many people
at the present day are prepared to admit), was able, in his very
full account of New Grange, to draw on George Coffey's
papers. In 1911 Coffey published his *New Grange (Brugh na
Boinne) and other incised Tumuli in Ireland*, which was based on
his earlier papers and is still the standard monograph on the
site. Anyone seriously interested in this monument and the
adjoining sites must refer to Coffey constantly. In writing this
book we have tried to think of ourselves as Coffey half a
century on, with the benefit of fresh lighting to see the stones

and their decoration, and with the benefit of half a century of archaeological research to attempt a reassessment of what New Grange was and what the Boyne tombs were in the history and prehistoric development of Ireland.

What has happened to New Grange since Coffey's time? In the first place the decorated basin that was in the central chamber in his time has been replaced in the north side chamber on top of the other basin, as it was described to be in the earliest accounts. In the 'thirties Professor R. A. S. Macalister, together with Dr Praeger and Mr Leask, re-exposed part of the kerb circle. They began with the fine decorated stone in front of the entrance, which they referred to as 'Stone 1' and worked round 'right-hand wise' until they had exposed fifty-four stones. There is no proper publication of this work, which is briefly referred to by Professor Macalister in his report on his work at Knowth. Here he describes how, when they had reached stone 54, 'the tenant interfered and owing to his objections the work had to be suspended.' By 'right-hand wise' Macalister appears to mean looking at the monument as though one came down the passage and stood at the entrance. Looking at the monument from outside, his exploration was clockwise and to the left, and he did not get round to stone *a*, at present exposed in the kerb circle.

Later trial excavations by Ó Ríordáin and Mr Ó hEochaidhe in the encircling stone circle near the entrance produced a few archaeological finds and information on the sockets of the stones. The interior of the passage and chamber is now illuminated very well by electricity and during the cutting of a trench for the laying of the electric cable a group of flints consisting of an adze and ten flakes was found south of the entrance by Mr Hartnett.

In the summer of 1962 Professor M. J. O'Kelly, under the auspices of the Board of Works, began excavations at New Grange to the north of the entrance. These revealed five stones

of the kerb circle, three of them decorated, and provided valuable information about the construction of the mound.

Before we leave the history of New Grange we must refer
to what may be the earliest mention of it and the other Boyne
tombs. In the *Annals of the Kingdom of Ireland by the Four
Masters* there is recorded the following incident under the year
A.D. 861; we quote from John O'Donovan's edition published
in Dublin, 1848–51:

> Amhlaeibh, Imhar, and Iailsi, three chieftains of the
> foreigners, and Lorcan, son of Cathal, Lord of Meath,
> plundered the land of Flann, son of Conang. The cave of
> Achadh-Aldai in Mughdhorna-Maighen; the cave of
> Cnoghbhai; the cave of the grave of Bodan, i.e. the shep-
> herd of Elcmar, over Dubhath; and the cave of the wife
> of Gobhann, at Drochat-atha, were plundered by the
> same foreigners.

In the *Annals of Ulster* the same incident is recorded under the
year 862, which we quote from the edition of the *Annals* edited
by W. M. Hennessy and B. McCarthy in Dublin 1848–51:

> The cave of Achadh-Aldai and of Cnodhba and the
> cave of Fort-Boadan over Dubabh, and the cave of the
> smith's wife, were searched by the foreigners, quod antea
> non perfectum est, viz. on the occasion when three kings
> of the foreigners plundered the land of Flann, son of
> Conaing, to wit Amhlaim, and Imhar and Auisle; and
> Lorcan, son of Cathal, King of Meath was with them
> thereat.

THE ORIGINAL NEW GRANGE

We have summarized the main accounts of New Grange before
the present day with a double purpose, first to find out whether
previous observers made a note of facts not observable today,

and secondly to chronicle what New Grange and the other tombs in the Boyne appeared to be to scholars and antiquaries from 1700 to 1950—Danish, Phoenician, Ancient Irish.

The history of the monument in historic times seems to be as follows: (1) it was broken into by the Danes in the ninth century; (2) it was discovered by accident in the late seventeenth century; (3) gold objects were discovered at the entrance in the mid-nineteenth century; (4) the Irish Board of Works under-took conservation work at the end of the nineteenth century, exposed the kerb circle, built a retaining wall and produced the bank and ditch effect; (5) Macalister and others in the 'thirties revealed again fifty-four of the kerb-stones; (6) small excavations later revealed a few finds and stone holes; (7) new excavations were begun by Professor O'Kelly in 1962, con-tinued in 1963, and will be taking place when this book is published in 1964.

How, then, should we envisage New Grange originally? In the first place the mound was probably considerably higher than at present—it has been used extensively as a quarry for stone: it was not tree-covered but probably entirely covered with white stones, and had a single megalith standing on top. Secondly, the mound would have been surrounded by a circle of standing stones, probably thirty-five in number. There was no bank and ditch surrounding the mound; the edge of the barrow was defined with visible kerb-stones, probably about a hundred of them carefully set with their tops at the same level, and perhaps as many as half of them bearing decoration. The entrance itself would almost certainly have been blocked with stones and earth and the entrance to the passage itself closed by the stone described by Wilkinson.

Inside we have to visualize the chamber without the present modern walls and supporting beams. We do not think that it is proved there was ever a pillar standing in the central cham-ber, although there might have been, and it seems likely that

the triangular section of the narrow part of the passage is not
as originally intended but is the result of the pressure of the
mound on the orthostats. This is as far as we can go in our
reconstruction of the original New Grange. The art which will
be described in the next chapter may have been painted, and
there may be other chambers in the mound not yet discovered,
but all this is speculation.

THE STONES

Coffey obtained a report on the stones used in the Boyne tombs
from R. Clark of the Geological Survey who said, 'The passages and chambers of the two mounds have been formed of
large slabs of the Lower Silurian rocks which crop up within
a few miles' distance. They were apparently either rudely
quarried for the purpose or split from surface rocks. With the
exception of some of the stones in the passage and others of the
upright course, the slabs in the interior of New Grange show
little traces of the original weathered surface of the rocks from
which they were taken, but, on the contrary, even faces, which
indicate that they have been split along the cleavage, and care
taken in their selection.' Clark goes on to discuss the stones of
the kerb circles at New Grange and Dowth and says, 'These
also are mostly derived from the Silurian rocks, interspersed
with a few varieties of traps. The parent rocks of the latter are
probably to be found amongst the igneous rocks which are
associated with the Silurian beds in the vicinity of the neighbouring town of Slane. In the outer circle at New Grange are
a number of standing stones mainly of Silurians (grits and
slates); a few traps also occur which may also be referred to the
Slane district.' Wilkinson had said that the upper basin in the
north side chamber was a granite from the Mourne district;
Clark thought it bore more resemblance 'to some of the
granites of the Wicklow series'.

CHAPTER II

The Art of New Grange

ONE OF THE MAIN REASONS for the fame and im⁄portance of New Grange is its richness in mural mega⁄lithic art. Six orthostats in the cruciform chamber, nine corbel stones of the chamber and one capstone—the roofing slab of the northern side chamber,—eleven orthostats in the passage, a false lintel over the main entrance, and three stones of the kerb circle are decorated; thirty stones all told, and when the kerb circle was investigated by the Board of Works they found that about half the total number of stones were ornamented although in many cases the decoration was slight—sometimes only a single spiral or zigzag. Thus New Grange probably has at least forty⁄five decorated stones of which thirty are now visible to us. These decorated stones make New Grange, quite apart from its size, the splendidness of its construction, and the excellence of its state of preservation, one of the most important megalithic tombs in Western Europe.

In richness of design and variety of motif as well as in the technical excellence of execution, New Grange can compare with only a few other megalithic tombs, of which Gavrinis in south⁄eastern Brittany is the main example that immediately comes to mind. These thirty or so decorated stones at New Grange are a very important component in any general picture of Irish megalithic art, or for that matter of the art of the megalith tomb builders of Western Europe as a whole. We deliberately say 'thirty or so' stones, not only because of the covered kerb⁄stones but because we do not claim that we have discovered all the megalithic art that is at present visible at New Grange. We have recorded several stones with decoration which were not listed by George Coffey, but we are still ready to be shown further stones with decoration, or motifs which we have missed on stones whose art we have already described. The study and recording of megalithic art depend very much on lighting, and although we have ourselves studied these stones on very many occasions in many lights, and have had the benefit of full notes from many others who have themselves studied the stones carefully on many other occasions, and full photographic records taken by several expert photographers on differing occasions, there may well be designs that we have missed. And this is of course quite apart from the possibility that future excavation, or the work of reconstruction of part of the mound, may reveal further examples of megalithic art. We are conscious too that in a tomb like New Grange which has been open to the general public for two hundred and fifty years there must be much recent 'art' in the form of names, initials and dates, and, we very much fear, some examples which copy earlier and authentic designs. There are on some surfaces triangles and lozenges which appear to us to be modern, and we have for that reason perhaps erred on the conservative side in our list of authentic examples of megalithic art.

Several of the sixty-odd orthostats which form the walls of passage and chamber bear cup-shaped depressions, and these cup-marks are recorded as and when they occur. This is not to imply that all the cup-marks are man-made; that some of them is beyond dispute, but others may be natural or may be slightly improved natural hollows.

The greater number of the orthostats used in New Grange have their surfaces prepared in some way or another. Clark noted that care had been taken to use stones split along their natural cleavages and said 'the spiral carvings have been cut exclusively on this description of stone.' There are stones with seemingly unprepared surfaces, but these are generally schistose or slaty stones whose surfaces might in any case be difficult vehicles for the portrayal of megalithic art. Most of the walling stones at New Grange provide ready surfaces for decoration when prepared. The two main techniques used for preparing the surface of the stones were *pocking* and *polishing*. Pocking produced a roughened but flattish surface, while polishing produced an even flat surface. The nature of these two finished surfaces can be well seen by looking at the photographs. Many stones bear surfaces that are polished as well as surfaces prepared by pocking, and the same stone may have unprepared surfaces as well.

From a very careful examination of all the stones it appears to us that the main sequence of techniques was, first to prepare the surface of the stone by pocking, and then to polish portions of it, but in some cases the sequence of techniques seems more complicated. Stone L. 19 for example, on the lefthand side of the passage, and one of the finest decorated stones in the tomb, *Fig. 10* bears fine ornament on a broad panel at eyelevel which has been polished; above and below this the surface of the stone has been pocked away, and at the base of the stone this pocking seems to have partly destroyed spirals already pocked on an earlier surface.

Two specialized techniques of surface preparation should be *Plates 13, 14* mentioned here. The first is best seen on stone R. 18 in the passage: the photograph shows clearly what look like marks where the chisel has cut away at the surface of the stone. These are the marks of a toothed chisel and the equivalent of the claw tool of the modern worker in stone. We can only here record these marks which have already been noted by others, but we cannot point to the survival of any bronze implement from New Grange or a comparable tomb which could have been used to produce them. The second specialized technique is best seen on R. 12 and consists of parallel shallow grooves or *Plate 8* channels; whether this is a technique of preparing the stone or of decorating it we do not know, but there can be no doubt of the objective existence of this channelling technique, which has been compared at various times with similar channelling at

Stonehenge and elsewhere. New Grange, like Stonehenge, is not a rude stone monument.

The three main techniques used in executing the decorative motifs at New Grange are (1) incised lines, (2) pocked lines, and (3) pocked areas. The pocked areas are mainly triangles and lozenges; at New Grange the dominant technique used is the pocking of lines and linear figures. Of course in pocking lines and grouped linear figures, other lines, areas and figures are reserved in between them, and it is often difficult to say in describing a particular stone what the design is really—four pocked lozenges arranged as two pairs side by side will naturally include by reservation an unpocked lozenge, and so on. One has only to look at some of the photographs to see that by incision or pocking the artists were trying to achieve a pattern, partly positive and partly negative, and that these patterns were mainly linear geometrical figures of zigzag lines, chevrons, triangles, lozenges, concentric circles, swags and spirals.

As far as we know there is no paint used in a decorative way at New Grange, though, as has been often pointed out, the pocked lines might originally have been keying surfaces for paint which has now disappeared. It has sometimes been suggested that the incised and pocked lines and surfaces were executed with metal tools, and this may be so; on the other hand it is quite easy to achieve the results with stone tools, particularly hard quartzite pebbles. Indeed, in view of the fact that the megalith builders of Ireland do not seem to have been metal-using at all times (or at least do not seem to have buried metal tools in their tombs), and that it is easier to simulate the results they achieved most convincingly by using quartzite pebbles and chisels, it seems reasonable to suppose, at least until the contrary is proved, that the art was executed with stone tools. This adds to our admiration of the technical excel-
Plates 17, 18   lence of the carving of, for example, stone L. 19 in the passage,

the famous stone at the entrance—surely one of the best examples of stone carving in pre-Roman Europe—and the roof
stone of the northern side chamber.

The question is often asked: were these techniques carried
out in the tomb, or before the stones were built into the tomb?
There has been considerable dispute on this point, and there
certainly are some designs (for example those on the edges of
R. 12 and L. 13) which could not have been done once the
stones concerned and the neighbouring stones were put into
position. Elsewhere there are designs on corbels which disap-
pear behind other stones, and on the underside of the corbel
stone behind C. 10 in the western side chamber are designs of
pocked lozenges and triangles which have only become visible
through stone C. 10 leaning forward. These and other designs
could never have been visible once the chamber and passage
were completed and must have been done before. This of
course does not mean that other designs were not done after
the tomb was completed or were not added during the time
when the tomb was being used sepulchrally.

It is now time, after these preliminary remarks, to take the
reader on a conducted tour of the tomb, pointing out the
decorated stones as we go. They are all marked in black on the
plan. Entering the passage from outside and looking first at the
left-hand side, we find no decoration on the first five orthostats;
L. 6, however, has a possible, rather doubtful cup-mark near
its base. There is no decoration on the next three stones; L. 10
has a smooth top part and a pocked lower part, and there are
marks on the top part which suggest that it was in process of
being pocked away or that someone was trying out his pocking
technique on it. It is possible that it has a faint chevron-like
design but we are inclined to think the resemblance to a
chevron pattern is fortuitous. The next stone up the passage,
L. 11, has a single shallow vertical groove cut down its length
on the right-hand half of the stone; L. 12 has a pocked chevron

Fig. 6

near the top at the right-hand side of the stone; L. 13 has no decoration on the surface of the stone facing the passage, but on the south edge facing the entrance is a pocked S-shaped figure and there are other indeterminate pocked figures up the side of the stone, and on the northern edge facing into the chamber three large pocked concentric circles (one may possibly be a spiral), not completely visible. L. 14 has no decoration; L. 15 has a row of three well-marked lozenges pocked on it—they are quartered and the triangles alternately pocked and left plain. L. 16 has no decoration; L. 17 has one well-marked lozenge at the middle near the top of the stone; L. 18 has no decoration.

Fig. 10. New Grange: the art on stone L.19

Plates 17, 18
Fig. 10

The next orthostat, L. 19, is one of the most famous stones at New Grange and has often been photographed and discussed. It is the stone, mentioned earlier, with a pocked-away top section, then a polished eye-level section with clear pocked decoration, and a lower section which has been pocked away, the pocking seemingly obliterating spirals now only faintly seen. The main decorated panel at eye-level (it is actually about

4 feet up) shows three spirals around a lozenge flanked on the left-hand side and framed above by zigzag lines forming a chevron pattern. Here there is a very clear sense of composition, and a definite plan to cover a surface for a special purpose. In the presence of this stone as in that of the roofing stone of the northern side chamber, and the great stone at the entrance of the whole tomb, we cannot speak of 'idle scribings' but of purposeful art, and it is no less purposeful because we cannot do more than guess at that old and hidden prehistoric purpose.

The next two stones, L. 20 and L. 21, have no decoration but the last stone on the left-hand side of the passage before the actual chamber begins (No. L. 22) has a design on a smooth polished surface of pocked chevrons on its left-hand side, as well as a double lozenge near its right-hand side. Coffey sug-gested that the pocked chevron pattern on the left-hand side of the stone was defined in a frame, but we suspect that the line he thought defined the frame on the right is really a crack in the surface. On the undressed surface of the stone is a pattern of lozenges and lines similar to the designs on C. 10, but we incline to the view that both these designs are modern imitations of old patterns.

Plate 20

Before entering the chamber with its rich ornament, let us go back to the entrance and walk up the passage looking at the stones on the right-hand side. The first two stones as one enters the passage have no decoration: R. 3 has at floor level a spiral of three turns, above it a pocked irregular zigzag line and above that a small spiral with indeterminate associated designs; there is also a spiral at the bottom left-hand edge of the stone, and towards the middle of the stone and 1 foot from present ground level a large but indistinct spiral of five turns. R. 4 and R. 5 have no decoration; R. 6 has six deep cup-marks on the south side of the stone varying in depth and size—the largest is 6 inches in diameter and 1 inch deep. The next five stones have no decoration. R. 12 has three horizontal grooves cut near the

Plate 8

bottom; on the right-hand edge of the stone facing the entrance is a series of pocked triangles and above this a small pocked design which has been mentioned by some writers as resem/ bling the eyebrows and nose motif seen in the mural and mobiliary art of the megalith builders; but we mention this suggestion here with no enthusiasm.

The next five stones have no decoration. R. 18 has an incised and pocked pattern of chevrons (the upper part incised and the lower part pocked) on its left-hand side; and on the right in the middle is the chisel marking to which reference has already been made. Coffey thought that the tool marks actually obliter/ ated the incised chevrons but it is more likely that they merely stop at the edge of the incised design. Above the incised chev/ rons and the tool marks are two badly incised double chevrons. On the back of the stone (and of course invisible when the tomb was intact) are two pocked concentric circles.

Stone R. 19 has some cup-marks and admirably demonstrates the difficulty of distinguishing between artificial and natural cup-shaped hollows. R. 20 has near the top of the stone on the left an oval hollow containing seven circles, one of which surrounds a cup-mark; underneath this is a circular hollow with three circles at least one of which is a double concentric circle. Below this is another rather vague hollow. The surface of this stone is heavily dressed back below a curving line about 1 foot from the top, the dressing being so done as to leave a median ridge 5 or more inches in width which curves down/ ward and to the right; this has suggested a face motif to some people but we think this is probably accidental.

Plates 19, 22   The last stone on the right of the passage (R. 21) has six ribs hollowed out across it and the surface of the stone has been pocked nearly all over, including the ribs. Below the ribs there is a deep oval cup and some small cups are to be seen at the edge of the stone. Near the top there is a design of halved lozenges (alternate halves being pocked) of rather irregular design. It has sometimes been pointed out that closely set parallel incised lines run horizontally over the upper part of this design and over the top portion of the stone; we do not think that these lines represent original designs but are most likely to have been where the original bedding planes of the stone have worn.

Let us now move into the chamber, beginning in the left-hand or southern side chamber. Stone 1 of the chamber (next to L. 22 of the passage with its chevrons) is undecorated, but the next stone, C. 2, has one large spiral above which are five lozenges and two triangles. The corbel immediately over this orthostat has its edge finely decorated with ten or eleven lozenges and zigzags forming an attractively composed linear pattern. C. 3 is the stone at the back of the southern side chamber and is decorated with three spirals; on the left-hand side of the right-hand spiral is a pocked design of an indeterminate kind, which has a faint resemblance to the horizontal zigzags or 'serpent' designs such as occur at Tara and Dowth. It is one of these spirals which Sir William Wilde thought was a plan of New Grange as a whole.

Plates 26, 27

Plates 15, 23

The next stone in our clockwise tour of this great cruciform chamber (C. 4) has on its face two spirals near the bottom right hand, and a small pocked design of an indeterminate nature near the top right-hand corner. At the bottom left is the curious pattern which was described by Coffey as a ship and which for convenience of reference we call 'Coffey's ship'. This is the pattern which Colonel Vallancey and Governor Pownall thought was writing, Vallancey taking it for Ogham, and Pownall for Phoenician. The 'ship' consists of a rough rectangle with eight internal cross lines, a short line outside and above the rectangle, and a circle (or the central circle of two concentric circles—there is trace of another circle) to the left of the main pattern. It is important to insist that this circle is to the left of the lined rectangle: the whole design has often

Plate 25

been interpreted and reproduced with the circle above the lined rectangle and the ship suggestion (which it should be remem-bered was a very tentative one of Coffey's) thus enhanced by a possible 'sun' motif over the ship. As to the interpretation of this motif we should prefer not to give any definite opinion: we are not at all convinced that it represents a ship, and it could possibly be one of the Breton buckler or *petit marmite* designs with cross-lines, but again it could well be something else. If we turn with a temporary sigh of relief to the edge of the stone, here again there is a puzzling motif: a central line with lines running off (representing a fern-leaf or a palm branch?), to the left of which at the base is a row of small chevrons. This motif is rare in the repertory of Western European megalithic art; it has been seen by some as a stylized human figure, but this must be regarded as a highly problematical interpretation.

Plate 24

Stones 5, 6 and 7 of the chamber have no decoration except that stone 6 has four possible (?) cup-marks in a row near its left edge and vague pocked designs above and slightly to the right of the middle of the stone, which might possibly be the beginnings of formal designs or the attempts of some mega-lithic artists to try out pocking technique. C. 8—the back stone of the west side chamber—has a pocked chevron on its top edge, a possible doubtful lozenge (it might be modern) to the left of this, and to the right of it near the top right-hand corner pocked triangles touching at their apexes and the re-mains of other pocked figures partly obscured by spalls between the orthostats at the corner.

One of the corbels at the back of the western side chamber—it is really the third corbel which forms the main capstone over this side chamber—has a lozenge pocked on its left side.

Plate 16

C. 9 has no decoration, but C. 10 is one of the most famous stones in New Grange. Low down on the stone are three spirals combined to form a triskele figure. Above this is a row of halved lozenges and triangles rather faintly marked. On the southern edge of the stone is a simple spiral and a small pocked oval. Behind this stone is a corbel stone, already referred to, which has only been revealed by the falling forward of C. 10, and on its underside is a design of pocked lozenges and triangles; these are cut on a surface which at the present day is one of the freshest and cleanest of the whole tomb—but of course this design could never have been seen by anyone using the tomb; it is an indisputable example of a secret design made and hidden away in the body of the structure.

Stone C. 11 has no decoration apart from bands of pocked surface in the form of a cross. But above this stone and as part of the corbelling is another with two or more triangles pocked and a reserved lozenge in between—the edge of the stone is broken and the precise design is impossible to determine. Between C. 10 and C. 11, and immediately under the broken stone with lozenges just described, is a corbel with pocked markings representing an indeterminate figure. C. 12 has no decoration, nor has C 13, but it appears to have been dressed in a series of narrow curved bands giving a rippled effect on the right-hand side. Stone 14 (the back stone of the northern side chamber) has no decoration, nor has C. 15 unless it be shallow cup-marks that run down the middle of the stone. Above this side chamber there are two decorated corbels; at the back of the side chamber the only corbel has an ornament of chevrons and triangles, and both ends of this stone, which is badly broken on the right, continue the ornament which runs in behind the structural stones of the mound. At the right-hand side of the side chamber is a corbel with six pocked lozenges very clearly marked.

Plates 31, 32

But the great glory of this side chamber from the point of view of megalithic art is the decorated underside of the capstone. This stone—which seems to us one of the most splendid stones in the whole megalithic mural art of Western Europe—is completely covered with ornament consisting of spirals, lozenges,

Plates 28-30
Fig. 11

arcs of circles (or swags), and concentric circles. There is also without doubt a motif representing in stylized form the oculi-goddess motif which appears so often in the mural and mobiliary megalithic art of France and Iberia. The edge of this splendidly decorated stone has a design of lozenges and chevrons raised against a pocked background.

Our tour of the art at New Grange inside the chamber comes to an end with stone C. 16, which has a design of lozenges and triangles on the edge of the stone facing towards the centre of the chamber, and stone C. 17, which has no decoration; lifting our eyes as we look out down the passage, the corbel over the opening comes into view, halfway from the beginning of the springing of the roof and the apex, with its triangles and halved lozenges alternately pocked and plain. But we must lower our eyes again, go back into the northern side chamber and look at the upper basin made of granite. On the western edge of this basin are two hollows and underneath them the traces of a channelled line of two semicircles; it is our opinion that this decoration may also represent the oculi-goddess motif.

Outside the chamber there are, as has been said, three decorated kerb-stones visible at present; they were labelled *a*, *b*

Plate 21

Plate 33

Fig. 12

Fig. 11. New Grange: the art on the underside of the capstone of the north side chamber

Fig. 12. New Grange: the art on (top) stone a, *and (bottom) stone* b *in the kerb circle (after Coffey)*

and *c* by Coffey. Stones *a* and *b* are to be seen in one of our drawings, and stone *b* is reproduced as a Plate. Stone *a* is at present heeled over and one has to lie on one's back to see the decoration; this consists of spirals, a raised lozenge pattern and concentric half-ellipses, surrounding motifs of concentric ellipses which themselves have cup-marks inside. Stone *b* has on its left side a design of pocked triangles and lozenges and on the right a double running spiral with two lozenges in between, and traces of other patterns including lozenges and concentric circles. Stone *c* is one of the most famous stones at New Grange,

Fig. 12
Plate 35

not only owing to its position at the entrance but by virtue of the quality of its workmanship and design. It is covered with a design of running spirals and lozenges, the whole executed with great skill in deep pocking, and having a very clear effect of a careful artistic composition. Above the entrance there is a false lintel with a horizontal pattern of halved lozenges executed in bold relief.

We have said that the operations of the Irish Board of Works in the 'nineties revealed a large number of decorated kerb-stones: this work went round New Grange in an anti-clock-wise fashion. In the 'thirties the excavations of Macalister and Leask working round in a clockwise fashion from the entrance revealed fifty-four stones of which ten were decorated. Macalister numbered these with the entrance stone (Coffey's *c*) as Num-ber 1. The other decorated stones were as follows: 2, small horizontal zigzag; 9, horizontal zigzag in double lines; 14, vertical zigzag line, ends returned to sinister side; 16, spiral, horizontal zigzag above; 17, spiral in upper dexter corner, two concentric circles; 20, cup-mark in the middle, five smaller cups on the sinister side; 22, a spiral, beneath it three cups in a horizontal row; 25, a spiral; and 26, a spiral. These particulars are taken from the brief list given by Macalister at the end of his Report on the Excavations at Knowth (*Proc. Royal Irish Academy*, XLIX, C, 150–1), which is the only account we have of this work.

In 1962 the excavations directed by Professor O'Kelly revealed three decorated kerb-stones to the right-hand side of the entrance.

We have now completed our description of the megalithic art at New Grange. Before analysing and discussing it we must see what art exists in the other tombs of the Boyne cemetery.

CHAPTER III

Dowth and Knowth

HIS CHAPTER IS CONCERNED with Dowth and
Knowth and the other monuments in the Bend of the
Boyne.

Plate 38

DOWTH

Dowth, or Dubadh, is about the same size as New Grange:
it is about 280 feet in diameter and 47 feet in height. Its base is
surrounded by a kerb of large stones as at New Grange but
there is no free-standing circle outside the mound (nor is there
one at Knowth). Sir William Wilde in his *The Beauties of the
Boyne* said of Dowth, 'although not so broad at the base as
New Grange, it was more conical,' and he draws attention in
writing and in a drawing reproduced there to the building on
the top of the mound, 'a modern structure, a *tea-house* erected
by the late eccentric Lord Netterville, and, certainly, although
his knowledge or love for antiquities may be questioned, there
can be no doubt of his having chosen a spot from whence could
be obtained one of the noblest prospects in Meath.'

Dowth was excavated in 1847 by the Committee of Antiquities of the Royal Irish Academy. It is not known when the
entrance to the tumulus was first discovered. The site had been
ransacked by the Vikings but exactly what they did or found
is not known. When Wilde first saw the site he noted a considerable gap in the western face of the mound much of which
he thought was caused by robbing stones for road-mending,
and he noted that this revealed a passage somewhat similar to
that at New Grange, adding, 'whether this passage was that
originally broken open by Amlaff and his plundering Danes
is difficult to determine.'

Coffey is very sharp in his comments on the 1847 excavations which were undertaken by a Mr Frith, whom he describes as 'one of the County Dublin surveyors'. Coffey goes on, 'Unfortunately no official record exists of the exploration of the tumulus by the Royal Irish Academy. Plans and drawings appear to have been made, but no trace of them can now be found. Indeed the mound was so pulled about by the explorers, and the work carried out with such doubtful wisdom, that the committee seem to have had a not unnatural shrinking from publicity.'

It seems best to quote here, as Coffey did, the account given by Wilde in his *Beauties of the Boyne*: 'Several excursions were made to the spot, for the purpose of deciding on the best means for gaining access to the interior, as from the analogy to New Grange, it was supposed to contain a central chamber. Opinions were divided as to whether a perpendicular shaft should be sunk from the top by a wellborer, or a horizontal tunnel driven in from one of the sides towards the centre. The remarkably loose material of which the mound is composed presented such objections to both these plans, while the apparent feasibility of obtaining ingress through the passage already open on the western side, so far, at least, as it was possible to follow it, was so inviting, that this latter plan was adopted. . . . A catacomb, a series of chambers not unlike those found beneath the great central chamber in the largest pyramid of the Sackara [*sic*] range . . . has been fully explored and rendered accessible to the curious. . . . Having made an open cutting in to the western side of the mound, in following out these passages it was certainly the most advisable as well as the cheapest plan to follow in the same course until the centre was reached. In effecting this the modern structure on the top was demolished: such however was indispensable and it may act as a warning and show all the future builders of teahouses, in such places, what may be the end of their labours.'

These excavations followed the passage into the central chamber with its cruciform plan. 'In the centre of the cham, ber', Wilde continues, 'stands a shallow stone basin or rude sarcophagus of an ovoid shape, much larger than any of those of New Grange, measuring five feet in its longer diameter. When the cave was recently opened, only a portion of this basin was discovered in its present locality, but all the frag, ments, nine in number, have since been recovered in the chambers and passages around. . . .' Wilde noted that there were no basins in the three adjoining recesses and describes the discovery of the curious extension to the southern side chamber that goes on to the south. He records that 'no central chamber was discovered, although the centre was reached,' and adds, 'it is possible however that there may be instead a number of minor crypts existing in the circumference of this great hill.'

Plates 39–41

The only record of what was found during the 1847 excava, tions at Dowth is contained in Wilde's account, in which he says, 'During the excavations some very interesting relics and antiquities were discovered. Among the stones which form the great heap or cairn were found a number of globular stone shot, about the size of grape,shot, probably sling stones, and also fragments of human heads: within the chamber, mixed with the clay and dust which had accumulated were found a quantity of bones, consisting of heaps, as well as scattered fragments of burned bones, many of which proved to be human; also several unburned bones of horses, pigs, deer, and birds, with portions of the heads of the short,horned variety of the ox, similar to those found at Dunshaughlin, and the head of a fox. Glass and amber beads, of unique shapes, portions of jet brace, lets, a curious stone button or fibula, bone bodkins, copper pins, and iron knives and rings, the two latter similar to those found at Dunshaughlin, were also picked up.' Wilde further adds that 'some years ago, a gentleman who then resided in the neighbourhood, cleared out a portion of the passages and found

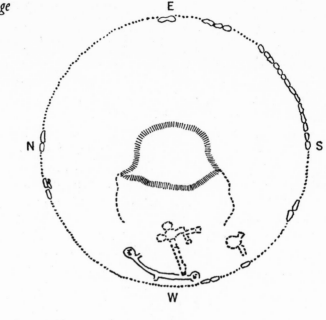

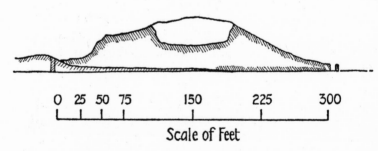

Fig. 13 (a). Plan and section of Dowth (after Coffey)

a few iron antiquities, some bones of mammals, and a small stone urn, which he lately presented to the Academy.'

In 1855 some further digging took place at Dowth under the direction of Sir Thomas Dean and there were discovered a souterrain and the southern Passage Grave. When visited

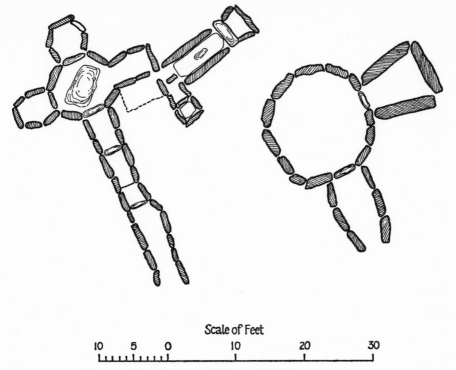

Fig. 13 (b). Detailed plan of chambers at Dowth (after Coffey)

today, then, Dowth consists of three separate structures: (1) the
souterrain of the late prehistoric or even protohistoric period,
and (2) and (3), two Passage Graves, the northern a fine example of a cruciform Passage Grave, while the southern is circular with one side chamber. It is proposed to refer to these as
Dowth North and Dowth South.

Unlike New Grange, neither of the Dowth Passage Graves
is corbelled but roofed with large capstones resting directly on
the heads of the orthostats (Dowth South has now a reinforced
concrete modern roof). Some of the orthostats at Dowth are
very large—up to 11 feet in height. The passage to Dowth North
is 27 feet long and leads into a central chamber 9 feet in

Fig. 13

diameter by 11 feet high. The passage is crossed by three sill‑stones and there is another one at the entrance to the central chamber; sill‑stones are also placed at the entrance to the east and north side chambers. At the end of the south side chamber is the curious extension which leads into a rectangular chamber 8 feet 6 inches long, floored by a great stone 8 feet long in the centre of which is a curious oval hollow. Two chambers open off this southern extension, one to the west and the other to the south; both are separated from the main long chamber by sill‑stones. The passage to Dowth South is 11 feet 6 inches in length and leads into a circular chamber 15 feet in diameter. On the south side of this there opens out a polygonal side chamber 9 feet long by 7 feet broad. Sill‑stones mark off the entrance from passage to central chamber and from central chamber to side chamber.

Plates 43, 44
One of the kerb‑stones on the eastern side of the mound is decorated with a pattern of rayed suns or wheels, and there is a spiral on the kerb‑stone at the entrance to the southern cham‑ber. The Passage Grave of Dowth North has several decorated stones in the passage and in the chamber. Only one of the
Plates 39-42
decorated stones in the passage has important markings; this is Stone 5 in Coffey's enumeration. The markings consist of concentric circles with a swag pattern underneath and an oval figure filled in with straight lines like a filleted fish; this is the fourth stone on the right hand going up the passage. The fourth stone on the left also has designs of concentric circles, and the fifth has circles and some indeterminate designs. In the chamber itself there are four stones with decorations. The stone on the left of the passage as one enters the chamber (No. 1 in Coffey's numbering) has on it a group of irregular concentric circles cut at about the middle of the stone. On the right of the passage as one enters the chamber (Coffey's Stone 4) is the most elaborately decorated stone at Dowth. It is decorated on two faces: the one opposite the passage has concentric circles

and a square/headed zigzag which has been described by some
as a serpent; on the face opposite the chamber are two clearly
marked spirals, rayed lines and patterns vaguely recalling the
fern/leaf and herring/bone pattern of New Grange. Across the
chamber is Stone 3 in Coffey's numbering, which is decorated
with rayed circles or wheels and spirals. Wilde described the
surface of this stone as pocked away to give relief to the carving,
but Coffey did not agree with this observation and neither do
we. Finally Stone 2, which is only 2 feet 6 inches high, has
on its surface facing the central chamber some cross and circle
markings, and some plain or concentric circles.

There are also some interesting decorated stones in Dowth   Plate 45
South. The stone on the left hand of the entrance to the main
chamber has a pocked circle design and another indeterminate
pattern. The main stone opposite the entrance in the chamber
has horizontal zigzags or chevrons on the left/hand side; Coffey
had noticed these on one visit, describing them as 'some good
bold chevrons . . .', but adding, 'on a subsequent visit I could
not find them, the stone appeared to be quite covered with
damp.' The next stone, on the left as one stands with one's back
to the passage, has on its left edge vertical zigzags with curved
ends precisely like those at Barclodiad y Gawres in Anglesey.
The right edge of the stone has faint traces of the same decora/
tion, but this stone as well as the previously described one has
suffered from damp and calcitic exudations. In the side cham/
ber of Dowth South there is one stone with decorations; it is
on the right hand of the chamber as one enters and is a large
stone 9 feet by 4 feet 6 inches. A large portion of the surface of
this stone has been prepared by pocking as at New Grange and
it is decorated with spirals, concentric circles, rayed circles, an
oval with a central line and side lines like a filleted fish, and
bears some other designs which seem to be modern imitations.
Coffey drew attention to designs on another stone—the lintel
stone above the entrance to the chamber. The upper surface of

Fig. 14. The alleged 'ship-markings' at Dowth according to Coffey

Fig. 14

this stone slopes back like a desk and on this surface Coffey thought he could identify cut on the stone 'three or four ships'. We cannot see these markings clearly and certainly not as ships, but we reproduce here Coffey's delineation of what he saw.

KNOWTH

Plate 37

Knowth is the third of the great mounds in the Boyne valley. Coffey gives it as 'nearly 700 feet in circumference or about 225 feet in diameter and between 40 and 50 feet in height'. He could find no traces of base stones although he thought they were 'possibly . . . covered by the sod, which is evenly grass-grown and makes it difficult to say exactly where the mound ends and the natural slope of the ground begins.' He continues, 'The mound is not open, nor is anything known as to whether it contains a chamber or not. It may possibly prove to be a blind cairn similar to the largest of the Loughcrew cairns described by Conwell. . . . At the northern side of the mound . . . some large stones showing above the surface of the ground seem to indicate the entrance to the tumulus: and as a cave at

Knowth is mentioned in the *Annals* as one of those plundered by the Danes in the ninth century, it is probable that the mound is chambered.'

These words of Coffey's were written in 1912, and to them Coffey added this admonition, 'It is to be hoped that no hasty attempt will be made to open this important tumulus.' In 1849 William Wilde had thus described Knowth: 'An abrupt hemispherical mound, with rather a flattened top. . . . Some enormous masses of stone, arranged in a circular manner round its base, tell us, however, that it is evidently the work of design. . . . As far as we can judge by external appearances, although history is against us, it appears to be as yet uninvesti-gated; but as there are no means of access to its interior, we can only speculate as to its use.' It is clear, then, that in 1849 as in 1912 there was no burial chamber visible and it is not certain to us that the entry in the *Annals* can be interpreted as meaning that the Vikings did break into the mound and actually find a chamber.

The late Professor R. A. S. Macalister has described how he visited Knowth on several occasions in the years before the 1939-45 war and was impressed by the large stones showing above the surface of the ground which Coffey had noted and which he thought perhaps indicated the entrance to the tumu-lus. Macalister wrote in 1943, 'Not only did they very strongly suggest to us, as to Coffey, the beginning of an entrance passage but on both occasions local information was obtained to the effect that this was commonly believed to be the entrance, and that it had been actually open until comparatively recent years; but was closed by a former proprietor to prevent cattle from straying into the chamber.' While recording this piece of local information Macalister said he had difficulty in accepting the statement without reservation owing to the testimony of Wilde, Coffey and others. He decided to find out what testimony the spade would provide, and excavated at Knowth in 1943.

Fig. 15

These excavations were concentrated on the apparent entrance to the chamber and the apparent kerb-stones: they also
revealed a souterrain on the summit of the mound. The excavation of the apparent entrance to the chamber defined a structure
whose plan as drawn by Macalister is shown here. In his
written account he says, 'The large stones were found to define
a cist; the parallel lines of smaller stones formed a passage running north and south, and leading into it; the cist was at its
northern end and separated from it by a kerbstone. The whole
is an entirely independent structure, having no connection
beyond mere juxtaposition with the mound of Knowth.' This
confusing account then goes on to refer to the structure as 'a
Passage Grave surrounded with a kerb of blocks of stone', and
in the published plan it is labelled as a Passage Grave. It
does not seem to us that this structure is still properly understood and indeed may be the entrance to a chamber, but what
is of special interest to us is the fact that six of the stones were

Fig. 15. Macalister's plan of Knowth from his 1943 Report of his excavations

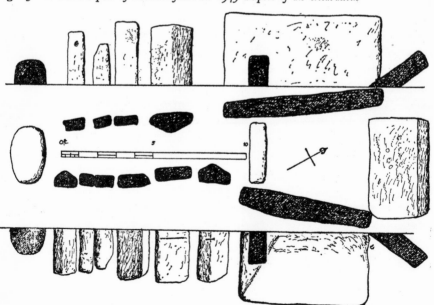

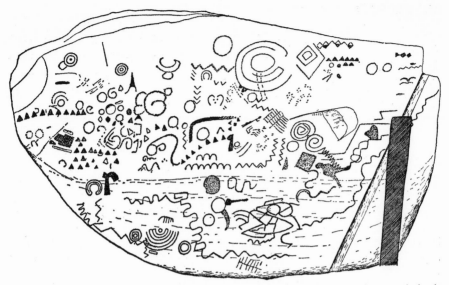

Fig. 16. Macalister's realisations of the designs on the east orthostat of the entrance to the Knowth chamber (his 'cist').

decorated with patterns of concentric circles, zigzags, and spirals. The large eastern stone in what Macalister described as the cist is heavily decorated: indeed Macalister himself went so far as to call it 'the most elaborately decorated stone of its size yet found in Ireland'. His drawing of it is reproduced here, and shows in addition to triangles, concentric circles, lozenges and zigzags, two unusual designs—a human figure and what looks like a hafted axe.

Fig. 16

The Macalister excavations were only able to uncover the kerb at Knowth for about half the way round; fifty-eight stones were found varying in length from 7 to 10 feet by 4 feet broad. Of these fifty-eight kerb-stones, forty-eight were decorated, and Macalister estimated that there might be as many as ninety carved stones in the kerb as a whole. The designs represented on these forty-eight kerb-stones include spirals and concentric circles, gapped circles, zigzags, wavy lines, and rayed circles

Plates 48, 49

Fig. 17

75

Fig. 17. *Macalister's realisations of the designs on four of the kerb-stones at Knowth*

or wheels. Two very unusual representations were commented on by Macalister: one was a design looking like an octopus and another one looking like a horned serpent. In publishing these designs Macalister was prompted to call them 'the most important collection of bronze-age carving yet found in Ireland if not in the world'. It would be a very fine thing if the whole kerb circle at Knowth could be re-excavated and preserved for all to see.

Macalister had some extremely interesting things to say about the technique of decoration on the kerb-stones at Knowth. Mr Leask had said to him that the decoration must have been first painted on the surface, being afterwards worked over with a pocking tool. He says that 'the downstrokes were broadened out as they naturally would have been in such brush-work, and this effect was faithfully reproduced in the pocked lines.' He notes that a chisel was never used and that all the patterns were made with a pocking tool. It was also noticed that some of the lines were bold and well-formed but that a few which were of an inferior technique 'betrayed the hand of a less expert artist.' In a final observation Macalister writes, 'Such differences in technique sometimes seemed to mark the work of two different craftsmen, whether in collaboration or in opposition—i.e. a later artificer modifying the work of a predecessor—could not always be determined . . . In some cases the ornament has been partly removed, to all appearance with intention.'

We have quoted extensively from the late Professor Macalister's report since it raises such interesting points about the form of the monument and the technique of decoration; and because in view of the covering-in of the stones again, it is the only document we have until Knowth is once more revealed.

THE BEND OF THE BOYNE

It is now time to consider the other earthworks in the neighbourhood of New Grange, Dowth and Knowth, but first we must refer to the stone structure immediately to the north of New Grange which was described by some as the cell of an Irish hermit, and by others as a 'grotto'—indeed it is so marked on Coffey's plan. It is surely a nineteenth-century ice-house, and like Lord Netterville's tea-house, of no further concern to us here.

The other earthworks in the Bend of the Boyne, or at least some of them, had been noted by earlier writers. Thus Governor Pownall recorded three other sites: first, 'a circle of unhewn stones set on end with the remains of a Kistvaen forming the north side thereof'—the diameter of the circle being 120 feet, the stones 5 or 6 feet high, and the monument, he thought, 'undoubtedly an erection of Druid superstition'; secondly, 'the *vestigia* of an oval camp which is certainly Danish,' and thirdly, 'a very large tumulus or barrow, under which (report says)

This also is in the same Field.

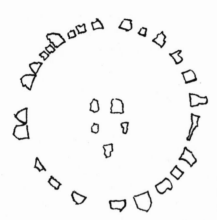

Fig. 18. A sketch by Anstis of a monument near New Grange (possibly K or L). (B.M. Stowe MS. 1024)

there is a cove like that at New Grange . . . It is . . . improved into a garden mount, planted with trees; and on the top of it is built a modern ornamental temple.' This account from Pownall's paper in *Archaeologia* for 1873 may refer to what we list below as Tumulus *K*, one of the circular earthworks and (?) Dowth itself. Colt Hoare in his description of New Grange referred to 'A large raised mound which bore a great resemblance to its elevated neighbour . . . a smaller sepulchral *tumulus*, that might easily be opened' in a field near New Grange and 'another raised earthen work nearer Lord Netterville's Park'—which is without doubt the large earthwork usually referred to as the Dowth fort.

We have already referred to the work of John Anstis in the early eighteenth century in the Bend of the Boyne and have *Figs. 8, 9* included his drawing of New Grange and of a decorated stone

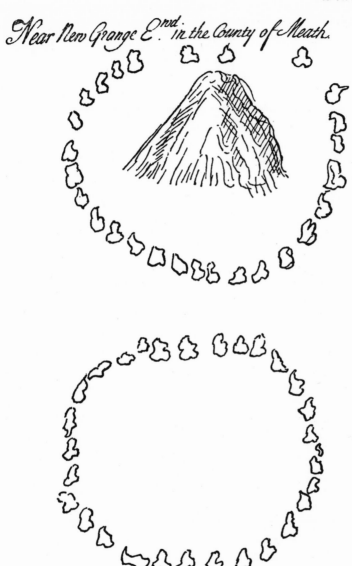

Fig. 19. Sketches by Anstis of sites near New Grange. (B.M. Stowe MS. 1024)

Figs. 18, 19

found in a lime kiln 'at New Grange'. The same collection of manuscript drawings, now in the British Museum (BM. Stowe 1024), also contains other drawings which we reproduce here but which it is not easy to identify with certainty with present-day monuments.

Coffey listed and mapped the various barrows and earth-works in the Bend of the Boyne and we have followed his listing and reproduce here his sketch plan with the addition of letters for the sites he called 'forts' and for the ploughed-out earthwork south of New Grange discovered by Professors de Valera and ÓRíordáin from a study of air photographs in 1953. (This is O on our revised plan.)

Fig. 20

Let us now go through the list of monuments. Coffey's *Tumulus A* is in the second field south of New Grange. It is built mainly of earth with large round stones embedded therein; there is no trace of a kerb circle. It is approximately circular in plan and conical in section with a slight depression on the top of the mound, but there are no signs which could definitely be said to be the result of plundering or excavation. In his descrip-tion of the site Coffey says, 'It appears to have been encircled, at a distance of about 200 feet from the mound, by a vallum, a portion of which is still traceable at the east side.' We found this bank visible to the north-east of this barrow, at about 220 feet from the mound, and that it has a very slight outer bank parallel to it; we could not find on the ground traces of this ring on the other sides of the mound. There is, however, some slight trace of a bank on the south which does not seem to fit in with the curve of the bank observed to the north-east of the barrow and cannot really be considered a part of it. To the north the circular earthwork joins up with an ancient field fence which continues at a tangent westward joining another modern field fence.

Plate 50

Tumulus B in Coffey's nomenclature is a large round barrow about 90 feet in diameter. There are no stones visible on the

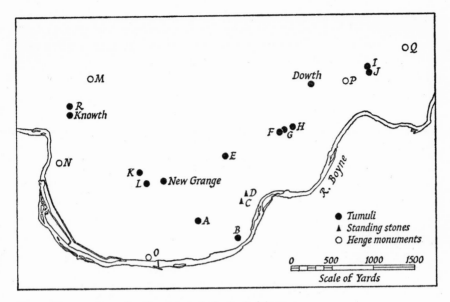

Fig. 20. Key map of mounds and earthworks in the Bend of the Boyne

surface but under a light capping of clay the mound seems to be largely composed of stone. The mound is conical in section; its sides are steep and well preserved. This mound is set on a flat expanse of land between the edge of the River Boyne and the edge of the low plateau some 300 yards away. Under present conditions it would appear that this mound or at least the platform on which it stands was liable to inundation during flood periods.

C and D on Coffey's numeration are single standing stones. C is a large stone of much weathered sandstone 10 feet high, 6 feet wide at the base and widening to 9 feet high at its greatest width at the top. Its site commands a wide view of the Boyne. D is a much smaller stone with a height of just under 6 feet, and is about the same dimension wide at its base. *Tumulus E* is a round conical-shaped mound slightly flattened on top (possibly due to soil slip) with no stones showing on the surface. The mound has very considerable traces of a kerb on all sides, with twenty stones clearly visible, and traces of many others partly showing through the sod. Some of the kerb-stones have slipped outwards. The slope of the mound flattens out considerably inside the kerb forming what might be called a berm about 16½ feet wide between the kerb and the rising of the mound.

Tumulus F in Coffey's scheme is an approximately circular shallow mound with a deep saucer-like depression in the centre. There are no stones showing in the mound itself which slopes gently to the surface level of the field. There are, however, some small stones visible beneath the surface especially on the inside of the depression. Two fairly large stones remain some 15 feet from the mound on the south side and there are several depressions on the south and east suggesting the position of other stones which have been removed—possibly the remains of a concentric circle.

Tumulus G is another rather large barrow but not a round barrow. It is generally accepted as an oval-shaped barrow, and in fact many take it to be a long barrow with its long axis from east to west. Crawford said guardedly that 'it has the appear-ance of being a long barrow' (*Antiquity*, 1927, 98). But the appearance of a long barrow can often be given by natural features and there is a strong possibility that this is a natural feature; only excavation will show. There is a fairly recent deep cutting in the centre of the mound on the north side, apparently for excavation or perhaps to get out some large stones for building, whilst several recent shallow trenches are to be seen in the western area of the mound. There is also a large stone rather less than 10 feet from the mound on the north-east and two depressions near the east end of the mound where stones have been removed.

Tumulus H is a round mound with a saucer-like depression inside giving the impression of a raised-up bank with a hollow flat space inside. The bank flattens out and forms an irregular step outside the mound to the south; it is made of earth and small stones. *Tumuli I* and *J* in Coffey's list are in the grounds of Dowth House, in the back lawn, an area generally known as 'The Pleasure Grounds'. Both are to the west side of the main monument at Dowth. *I* is a round low mound overgrown with huge trees; there is a shallow depression in the centre of the mound, and the remains of what may have been a kerb directly outside the bank at the bottom of the slight slope of the bank. It is represented by four large stones which touch on the west side and by several others on the periphery. There are no apparent traces of chamber or passage.

Tumulus J is 60 yards from *I* and is in an overgrown garden: Coffey described it as a round mound with a clearly defined edge probably due to its use as a daffodil bed. Today it is thickly overgrown, and its central structure is locally known as 'the old ice house'. This is a corbelled chamber in the centre of the mound which may be entered through the open roof; Coffey noted a capstone lying some distance from what he presumed to have been its original position. The chamber is divided by projecting and free-standing uprights into compart-ments. There are no traces of a kerb and the position of the passage is not evidenced in the chamber itself but a great deal of the chamber in the north-east is covered by a deep deposit of clay which has washed into it and makes examination and planning very difficult. Coffey's description of this chamber is worth quoting: 'A corbel-roofed chamber, formed of flags laid on the plan of an irregular hexagon. The chamber thus formed is about 8 feet high and 10 feet in diameter. Five cells are placed around the sides, formed by small flags set on end; no trace of a passage is apparent; none of the stones are in-scribed.' Looking down into the burial chamber at the present day is rather like looking into the ruined corbelled tombs at Alcalá in southern Portugal which may well be the ancestors of the Boyne tombs; this tumulus *J* is certainly the monument in the Boyne complex which most demands excavation.

Coffey's inventory finished with *J* but we have numbered the other barrows and earthworks to be described, beginning with the two mounds immediately to the west of New Grange itself, which we are calling *K* and *L*. Tumulus *K* is to the west of New Grange and is the monument described by Sir William Wilde when he said he was present 'at the opening of a small kistvaen, reached by a narrow stone passage—a sort of minia- ture New Grange' on the western slope of the natural hill on which New Grange stands, and he records that in it were found a quantity of animal bones and human bones, some burned, and he also alleged there was evidence that 'the victim, or the dead body, was burned within the grave.' Traces of this chamber survive and it looks like a construction with a fairly long passage and a chamber at the northern end, and an en- trance seemingly at the south-east as at New Grange. The mound is apparently encircled with a retaining kerb which appears clearly all the way round except for a short breach at the eastern side. The stones of the kerb, which does not appear to be concentric with the passage, are in the main covered over with earth but a few moss-covered stones appear above the surface. The side walls of the passage are clearly visible, con- sisting of fairly long slabs set on edge, and an end stone appears lying across the entrance at the south. All that remains of the chamber is an accumulation of stones at the northern end, most of which are covered with grass and earth. Outside this kerb the ground slopes gently away on all sides except on the east where it joins up with a second hill, and it is on this eminence, west of New Grange and between New Grange and Tumulus *K*, that there is what many people have described as another tumulus and which for convenience of reference we are calling Tumulus *L*. It has a very indefinite outline and may well be a natural mound—but at the centre there is a small depression

Fig. 21

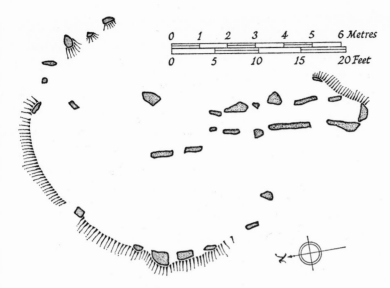

Fig. 21. Plan of site K at New Grange

filled with loose stones, and when these were removed they revealed a stone at a depth of 14 inches.

This survey shows, then, that in the Bend of the Boyne there are thirteen sites of which two may be natural (*G* and *L*), of which four have certainly burial chambers (New Grange, Dowth, *J* and *K*) and one, Knowth, almost certainly has a chamber not yet discovered. It is of course by no means certain that all these sites cover chambered tombs; some of the mounds may date from a later period. It is, however, inherently prob‑ able that not only Knowth but several of the other mounds cover burial chambers and that we may refer to all of them without impropriety as the Boyne cemetery of chambered barrows. Recently Dr George Eogan excavated one of the smaller mounds near Knowth, revealing a burial chamber with stones decorated in the New Grange style.

Fig. 22

But there are earthworks other than barrows in the Bend of the Boyne which should be noted here. We have continued

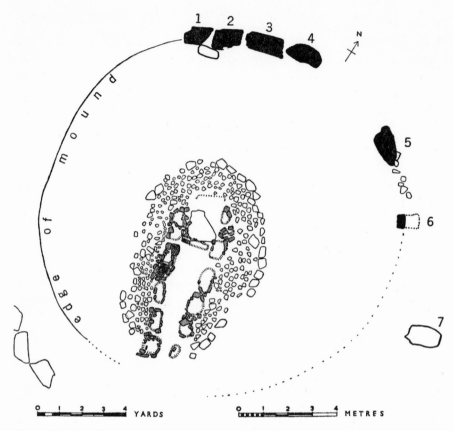

Fig. 22. Plan of smaller monument at Knowth (after Eogan)

Plate 53

numbering them in Coffey's sequence. First, there are two 'forts' near Knowth. The first is on low-lying marshy land to the north-east of Knowth House (*M*). It is a large circular earthwork surrounded by an inner bank with a ditch outside this and a relatively low outer bank. The interior has an un-even surface and is raised somewhat above the level of the surrounding marshy field. There are no remains of any struc-tures visible inside the earthwork. The second 'fort' near Knowth is about half a mile to the south-west; it is directly above the banks of the Boyne on a hill, and enclosed by a slight inner bank, ditch and slight outer bank (Site *N*).

Site *O* is not on Coffey's list of sites and was discovered on an air photograph taken in 1953. Now that it has been located Plate 51 from the air it is easy to see it clearly on the ground and indeed in special conditions of lighting it can be seen from New Grange itself, whence it is about half a mile distant. Though ploughed in, it was originally a very large circular bank; it is suggested that the entrance was on the south-east but this is no more than a guess at the moment. This is a site like *M* and *N*; its diameter was between 120 and 150 yards and the present maximum width of the bank is about 60 yards.

Near Dowth House there are two circular earthworks des-cribed as 'forts', which we have labelled *P* and *Q*. *P* is a small earthwork midway between the Dowth chambered barrow and Dowth House. *Q* is to the east of Dowth House and is a large Plate 54 circular earthwork with an opening in the bank at the south-west and another at the north-east. What are these five circular earthworks which we have labelled *M, N, O, P, Q*? They are marked on maps—or at least four of them—as 'forts', but this is no more a careful diagnosis than the fact that some of the Boyne barrows are labelled 'moats'. *Q* is a very large and impressive earthwork with a diameter of between 420 and 450 feet. ÓRíordáin, writing about the discovery of site *O*, said that only two possibilities existed; these circular earthworks are either ring-forts or ritual enclosures. Macalister in his *The Archaeology of Ireland* (1928) suggested that earthwork *O* at Dowth might have been 'a kind of theatre in which some of the burial rites could take place'. It is worth recalling that we do know some examples of what must be circular ritual en-closures in Ireland: the Giant's Ring, County Down, is one, and it surrounds a megalithic tomb; Longstone Rath, County Kildare, is another surrounding a grave and standing stone, and there are also the bank-and-ditch monuments on the

Curragh, and the embanked stone circle at Lough Gur. There is a large circular enclosure with a ditch inside the bank near the chambered tombs of Fourknocks. It does seem to us that it is no longer possible to deny the existence in Ireland of circular ritual enclosures comparable in a general way to the henge monuments and stone circles of Great Britain, and that in the Bend of the Boyne we have not only a collection of remarkable tombs, but a collection of remarkable temples. And if this should seem too extravagant a statement, may we quote the reservation made when the discovery of earthwork O was published: 'One must remain content with indicating the possi-bilities; only excavation could reveal the purpose of this earth-work and tell us whether its intriguing position in proximity to the Boyne tombs is, in fact, significant.'

A campaign of excavation is much needed in the next fifteen years in the Boyne area. It should not only reveal the date and purpose of the so-called 'forts', but should aim at re-revealing and preserving the whole kerb circles at New Grange, Dowth and Knowth, should discover the chamber or chambers at Knowth, should determine the plan and form of the chamber tomb *J* with its corbelled roof, and perhaps also tell us what tumulus *B* is.

Three sites require brief mention before we leave these addi-tional monuments in the Boyne area. In his *Beauties of the Boyne*, Wilde referred to a site called Cloghlea which was in the same field as the 'fort' at Dowth—our site *Q*—and des-cribes it as 'a portion of a stone circle evidently a part of the side wall or basement of a sepulchral chamber similar to New Grange, than which it is, perhaps, even larger.' Wilde describes how four of these stones 'of immense size (one twelve feet long)' were still standing and 'two others are prostrate, and two more lying in the adjoining quarry—eight in all.' He goes on to say, 'Human remains have, on more than one occasion, been found in the vicinity of this remnant of an ancient tumulus. On the

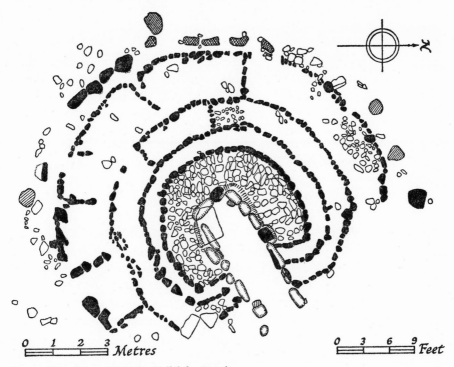

0   1   2   3   Metres

0   3   6   9   Feet

Fig. 23. Plan of site at Towneley Hall (after Eogan)

edges of these stones will be found identations similar to those in some of the stones of the passage of New Grange,' and here he is presumably describing the grooves on R. 21. Pownall also saw this circle at Cloghlea and at that time there were eleven stones in position. He remarks, 'I paced this circle, and as well as I recollect it, it is not above 21 feet. The stones are large and massive, and about 5 and 6 feet high. There remain eight of these stones together in one part of the circle: two in another part and one by itself. On the left hand from the entrance into the circle lies a flat stone which seems to have been either the top of a kistvaen or a small cromlech.' Coffey's comment was, 'The remains of this monument are still to be seen though I could not make out all the stones mentioned.' Neither could we; Cloghlea remains a mystery.

The second of these sites is at Monk Newton, less than 2 miles north of Knowth; here is a badly damaged tumulus referred to as a 'moat' on the Ordnance Survey map. The mound is badly overgrown with trees and bushes—there is a deep excavation on the east side down to nearly field level, and lots of small stones occur in this hollow. This site may well be another Boyne chambered tomb.

The third and last of these additional sites is in the grounds of Townleyhall, about 2 miles east of the Monk Newton 'moat'. It is situated on the highest point of a low ridge and before excavation it appeared as a low, flat-topped and roughly circular mound about 3 feet high and 55 feet in diameter. The site was excavated in 1960 and 1961 by Mr Frank Mitchell and Dr George Eogan of the Department of Archaeology, Trinity College, Dublin. The barrow was revealed to have four settings of stones and to be an Entrance Grave or Undifferentiated Passage Grave of which only two stones remained *in situ*. The other stone holes were recovered and the plan determined. No finds were made in the chamber but it appears that the funerary structure had been built on a Neolithic habitation layer which produced worked flints (hollow scrapers, thumb and side scrapers) and pottery with cord ornament, stab and stab-and-drag impressions, and lightly incised lines—in fact what Professor Gordon Childe called Carrowkeel ware.

Fig. 23

This now concludes our survey of the Boyne tombs other than New Grange, Dowth and Knowth. Before we can address ourselves to the questions about the significance, purpose, and date of these Boyne monuments we must widen our inquiry and see where in the British Isles we find comparable tombs, and also where we find comparable art. Only then shall we be able to discuss in their full contexts the many problems still raised by New Grange and the tombs in the Bend of the Boyne. The next chapter is devoted to studying this comparative evidence from Ireland and Great Britain.

CHAPTER IV

The Irish and British Passage Graves

THE GREAT CEMETERY of Passage Graves in the Bend of the Boyne which has been described in the first three chapters of this book is only one—though admittedly the finest —of four such cemeteries in Ireland. The other three are Lough-crew in County Meath, and Carrowmore and Carrowkeel in County Sligo. In addition to these cemeteries of Passage Graves there are isolated occurrences of one or two Passage Graves at thirty-seven other sites in Ireland; three of these comprise two sites (Saggart Hill, Slievethoul in County Dublin; Knockin-gen, Gormaston Townland in County Meath, and Four-knocks, also in County Meath). The distribution and location of these sites is shown on the map. The total number of Passage Graves in Ireland is somewhere between a hundred and fifty and two hundred; this must be a general estimate because of the uncertainty of various sites.

Fig. 24

There may well be more sites—perhaps many more sites—of Passage Graves in Ireland awaiting discovery. Fourknocks was not discovered until 1949, and the Mound of the Hostages was revealed to be a Passage Grave only by the excavations of 1957. We can only guess at the number of Passage Graves that have been destroyed since prehistoric times. In various parts of Europe we know that the destruction of megalithic tombs in historical times has been very considerable. For example the Baltic island of Rügen, which apparently had two hundred and twenty-nine megalithic tombs in 1827, had only forty in the 1930s. The *Landkreis* of Uelzen, which had two hundred and nineteen tombs in 1846, had only seventeen in the 1950s. It is

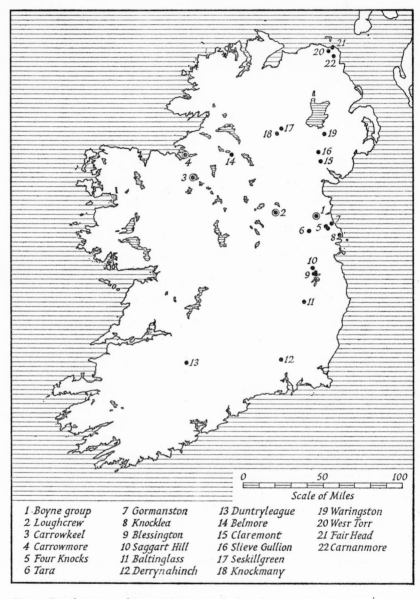

Fig. 24. Distribution map of Passage Graves in Ireland

1 Boyne group	7 Gormanston	13 Duntryleague	19 Waringston
2 Loughcrew	8 Knocklea	14 Belmore	20 West Torr
3 Carrowkeel	9 Blessington	15 Claremont	21 Fair Head
4 Carrowmore	10 Saggart Hill	16 Slieve Gullion	22 Carnanmore
5 Four Knocks	11 Baltinglass	17 Seskillgreen	
6 Tara	12 Derrynahinch	18 Knockmany	

unlikely that there has been anything comparable in the destruc⁄
tion of Passage Graves in Ireland; we doubt whether there
were ever more than two hundred and fifty Passage Graves there.
Of the Passage Graves in Ireland, in addition to New
Grange, Dowth and Knowth, nine sites have decorated stones,
namely Fourknocks, Tara, Loughcrew, Seefin, Baltinglass,
Carrowmore, Carnanmore, Knockmany and Seskillgreen. The
distribution of these sites is shown on the map. The simplest   *Fig. 25*
way to appreciate the variety and content of these decorated and
undecorated Passage Graves in Ireland is to describe them geo⁄
graphically in relation to the Boyne tombs, and from this point
of view they fall geographically into three: those to the south of
the Boyne, those east of the Boyne, and those north.

THE SOUTHERN TOMBS

The Fourknocks sites 10 miles to the south of Drogheda and
15 miles as the crow flies south⁄east of New Grange. Three
mounds were excavated here in 1950–2 by Mr P. J. Hartnett.
Fourknocks I is a cruciform Passage Grave in a circular mound   *Fig. 26*
60 feet in diameter and 12 feet high; it had a dry stone wall
instead of a kerb of megaliths. A short passage leads into a
large central chamber with a maximum diameter of 20 feet out
of which open three side chambers. The walls survive to about
two⁄thirds of their original height, beginning with orthostats
and then continuing with oversailing corbels. The excavator
was of the opinion that the final roof was of timber supported
by a central pole, the socket for which was found. Twelve of
the structural stones in the main chamber and entrance passage
were decorated in the style we have come to know in the Boyne
tombs with face⁄motifs, spirals, zigzags, triangles, circles and
cup⁄marks.

Mr Hartnett drew attention to a very interesting technical
detail in his study of Stone 4 at Fourknocks I, in which he says

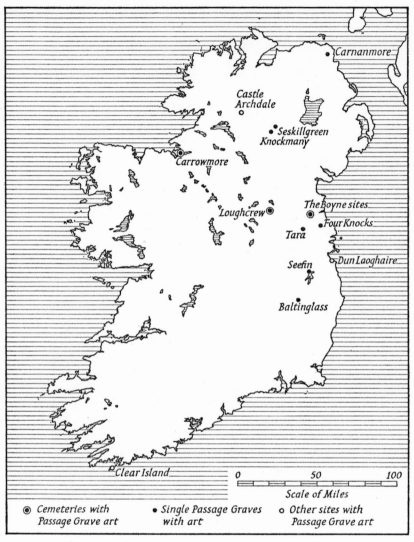

Fig. 25. Distribution map of Passage Grave art in Ireland (after Powell, revised). Encircled dots represent cemeteries with more than one decorated Passage Grave

that the artist's blue-print can be clearly seen on the face of the stone consisting of a framework of lightly incised verticals five in number spaced at equal intervals running from the top of the stone to very nearly ground level and linked by parallel lines of zigzags. 'Having completed his layout,' wrote Hartnett, 'the artist apparently began to peck out alternate bands in the first three columns leaving the intervening bands untouched. In the fourth column the pecked bands do not coincide with those on the first three, but whether this was intentional or not cannot be determined. What does appear to have been a slip-up, however, occurs near the upper end of column 3 where two adjacent bands were pecked. It may be assumed that what the Bronze Age artist had in mind was to produce a pattern of ribbon-like chevrons in false relief and that, because of a mistake in the early stages, the full scheme was never completed.' This interpretation of the decoration on this stone, with which we entirely agree, throws an intimate light on the actual technique of Boyne art—beginning with the incised lines and then being followed up by pocking with a pointed quartzite pebble.

As can be seen from the examples included here much of the art work at Fourknocks I is very good chevron and lozenge patterning. Two stones, however, are of very special and unusual interest; these are Stone 7 and Stone a. Stone 7 is one of the functional uprights of the chamber and has a design which has been interpreted as anthropomorphic; indeed it was referred to by the workmen on the excavation as 'The Clown', or 'The Old Man of Four Knocks', or even 'King Tut'. Mr Hartnett thinks it belongs unquestionably to the anthropomorphic group of statues-menhirs. It certainly has a resemblance to them but also to the decorated stone at Barclodiad y Gawres. Stone a was found outside the burial chamber, and may have been moved out in historical times. It has now been set up in the chamber. On its edge there is a chevron and lozenge pattern but on its face a design of spiral and curvilinear patterns which again has been interpreted as anthropomorphic. In his report of his excavations Hartnett says, 'The writer has no hesitation in

Plates 58–60, 62, 64

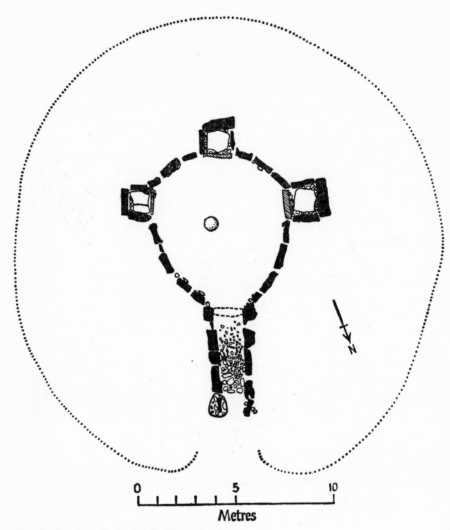

Fig. 26. Plan of Fourknocks I (after Hartnett)

ascribing this to the anthropomorphic group of passage grave art. He would go further and interpret it as an "impressionist" representation of a rather animated female figure with plenty of movement expressed by swirling spirals and curves.'

No art was found in the other two mounds excavated at Fourknocks; Fourknocks II seems to have been a purely ritual structure contemporaneous with the Passage Grave for which it may have served as a crematorium. Fourknocks III covered a central cremation cist of the Middle to Late Bronze Age.

Tara is even more famous as an ancient site than New Grange and the Boyne monuments—indeed Tara, Royal Tara, Tara of the Kings is perhaps the most famous site in ancient Ireland. It lies about 10 miles just west of south of New Grange, 12 miles west of Fourknocks and just over 20 miles north-west of Dublin. The various earthworks here have been given names in an attempt to identify them with the history and early tradi, tions of Ireland; one is the Banqueting Hall, another the Rath of the Synods—so called, we are told, because of the Synods held there by St Patrick, by Saints Brendan and Ruadhan and by St Adamnan, and a third the Mound of the Hostages. Excavation at the Mound of the Hostages was commenced by Professor ÓRíordáin in 1955 and 1956 and completed in 1959 by Professor R. de Valera. Before excavation it seemed to be no more than a grass-grown mound 70 feet in diameter and 9 feet high. Most people imagined that the excavations would reveal features of an antiquity no greater than, say, the beginning of the Christian era, but in the first two seasons there were found some forty Middle Bronze Age burials placed as secondaries in the mound. All except one were cremations and the one was the body of a young man of fourteen to fifteen years of age laid in a flexed position, with around his neck an elaborate necklace of bronze, amber, jet and faience.

Below these secondary burials there was discovered a megali, thic Passage Grave 13 feet long by 3 to 4 feet wide and 6 feet in height walled by orthostats and roofed by capstones. The second stone walling the southern side was decorated by pock, ing; the designs include concentric circles, a serpent-like zig, zag, some concentric half-ellipses, and two opposed semicircles.

West of the Tara and Fourknocks sites there are other sites of Passage Graves at Knockingen, Gormanston Townland (two sites), Bremore Townland and Saggart Hill, Slievethoul Townland (two sites). South of Dublin on the northern edge of the Wicklow or Dublin mountains are some nine barrows of which five certainly contain Passage Graves, namely Seehan Mountain, Knockanvindee, Saggart Hill in Crockaunadree‑nagh Townland and Seefigan. Another site sometimes included in these lists is Tibradden: it has often been claimed as a genuine Passage Grave and we certainly thought it one for many years. It is in fact a nineteenth‑century folly of a rather special kind. Before the excavation of the site by the National Monuments Branch of the Office of Public Works in Ireland, it was thought that the barrow on Tibradden mountain con‑ tained a dry‑walled Passage Grave of classic form, and that in the centre of the circular chamber there had been found in 1849 a megalithic cist containing a food vessel and cremated bones. Before the clearance work done by Mr Marcus Ó hEochaidhe three years ago the site had indeed the semblance of a filled‑in Passage Grave, but now that it is open down to ground level this semblance is revealed as accidental. The whole construc‑ tion of passage and chamber is uncharacteristic of the megalith builders and there is built around the inside of the chamber a stone bench. Mr Ó hEochaidhe is of the opinion that passage and chamber were built in the mid‑nineteenth century, and we can imagine visitors then sitting on the stone seat and admiring the central cist.

In his pioneer survey of the Irish Passage Graves, on which the information in this section is based, Mr T. G. E. Powell lists a small group of sites extending south and south‑west from the Wicklow sites; they include Baltinglass, Derrynahinch and Duntryleague.

At least two of these sites—Seefin and Baltinglass—have some decorated motifs, and the designs at Seefin bear striking

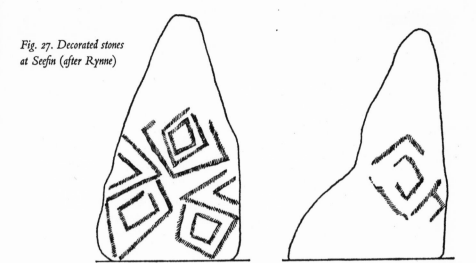

*Fig. 27. Decorated stones
at Seefin (after Rynne)*

likenesses to the decorated stones 2 and 5 and 22 at Barclodiad
y Gawres in Anglesey. From Clear Island in County Cork
comes an isolated slab decorated in the style of megalithic art.
There is no certainty that this stone was ever part of a megalithic
tomb, but in style and execution it is one of the best examples
of megalithic mural art in Ireland.

Fig. 27
Plate 65

TOMBS WEST OF THE BOYNE

On a line from the Boyne to Sligo Bay are to be found three
great cemeteries of Passage Graves. The cemetery of Carrowmore near Sligo itself has (or had) about sixty-five Passage
Graves and it seems probable that there were originally many
more; indeed Carrowmore is one of the largest concentrations
of megalithic tombs in Europe. The cemetery, situated about
2 miles south-west of Sligo Town, extends over an area roughly
1 mile from north to south by half a mile from east to west.
There are no corbelled structures here; all the tombs are walled
with rough orthostats and roofed with capstones resting directly
on the heads of the orthostats. Carrowmore itself is overlooked

by the mountain of Knockarea which is crowned by the very large unopened cairn of Misgaun Meav; it is about 200 feet in diameter and may well contain a Passage Grave. Around it are smaller mounds containing denuded Passage Graves.

The Carrowkeel Passage Grave cemetery is about 15 miles south of the town of Sligo, on the Brickleve Mountains immediately west of Lough Arrow. These mountains reach a height of 1057 feet; the Carrowkeel cemetery is on the eastern side of the mountains where the top is broken up by a series of rifts; the fourteen barrows are on the ridges, many of them at the highest point of the ridge. The whole cemetery was excavated by Macalister, Armstrong and Praeger in 1911 and in their published report they show a feature which if true would be a great surprise in megalithic architecture, namely that the megalithic chambers were constructed not on ground level but in the body of the mound. This is almost certainly an error of observation and surveying, and the confusing of the level of the skirts of the mounds with the floor of the chambers which are anyhow set on natural rises. The same false observation of levels was made by Cartailhac in studying megalithic barrows in the Aveyron department of southern France.

The Loughcrew Hills are only 25 miles west of New Grange, and 2 miles south-east of Oldcastle in the extreme west of County Meath. They are a ridge of hills 3 miles long extending in an east–west direction with three main summits, Carnbawn on the west, Sliabh na Caillighe (The Hag's Mountain) in the centre and Patrickstown Hill on the east. The hills attain an average height of between 800 and 900 feet; the hill of Sliabh na Caillighe itself reaches a height of 904 feet and commands a wonderful view of part of the great central plain of Ireland. The individual name of this central hill is sometimes given to the hills as a whole. The hills originally contained a cemetery of about thirty round mounds; by now some of these have been destroyed or ruined but many including the largest remain.

The Loughcrew barrows were discovered in 1865 and most of them at that time surveyed and partly excavated by a teacher in the local elementary school, by name Eugene Alfred Conwell who numbered them in a series from A to Z. Conwell thought that Tomb T, from a distance the most conspicuous of the cairns and crowning the summit of Sliabh na Caillighe, could be identified as the Tomb of Ollamh Fodhla. Conwell listed fourteen cairns on Carnbane and seven (including T) on the top of the central mountain. Of these monuments thirteen have decorated stones; Conwell wrote, 'In all I have laid bare 1393 separate devices.'

Plates 36, 56, 57, 66–68

TOMBS NORTH OF DUBLIN

In his survey of Irish Passage Graves T. G. E. Powell lists a group of sites in Armagh such as Carnvaddy, Clarmont, Slieve Gullion and Vicars Carn in Carnavanaghan Townland, Waringstown, Slieve Donard and a site on Colin Mountain in Ballycolin Townland, a group of five sites in north Antrim (which he describes as his Ballycastle or North Antrim Group) comprising Carnanmore, West Torr, Fair Head, Crockatreemore and Carnantruagh, and five sites between Lough Neagh and Lough Erne, namely Belmore Mountain, Castle Archdale Deerpark, Knockmany, Shantavnt Scotch and Seskillgreen. Two of the sites in this last group, Seskillgreen and Knockmany, have interesting engravings. At Seskillgreen, and immediately to the south-east of the Post Office, are the remains of a megalithic burial chamber of oval shape about 11 feet in length and 7 feet 6 inches broad. The faces of several of the uprights are carved, and the two particularly interesting stones are at the back of the chamber. They are decorated with concentric circles and lozenges. Not far away another megalithic slab was found decorated with concentric circles, rayed designs and cup-marks clearly in the

Plate 63

tradition of Irish Passage Grave art, and probably the remains of another Passage Grave.

Knockmany is 2½ miles north of Clogher in the county of Tyrone and is on a hill overlooking the Blackwater at a height of 779 feet. It consists of a rectangular chamber measuring 14 feet by 6 feet in a large circular barrow 70 feet in diameter.

Plate 61

Three of the walling stones of the chamber are decorated and two of these have very interesting patterns. One (Coffey's Stone *A*) has concentric circles, zigzags, tight curved-ended zigzags like squibs, triangles and in the middle of the stone a design which is surely the oculus-goddess pattern. Stone *D* is rather like one of the kerb-stones described and drawn by Macalister at Knowth, with concentric circles, concentric half ellipses, the curved 'squib' zigzag which some have described as a serpent, and other patterns.

There are also some motifs at the site of Carnanmore, as well as in the curious site of Millin Bay.

PASSAGE GRAVES IN GREAT BRITAIN

We must now extend our survey of Irish Passage Graves, which began with the Boyne cemetery, to other parts of the

Figs. 28, 29

British Isles. Across the Irish Sea in Anglesey are two monu-ments of Passage Grave type namely Bryn Celli Ddu and Barclodiad y Gawres; in Wales too there are some half-dozen or so megalithic tombs, like Presaddfed and Ty Newydd in Anglesey, Ystum Cegid Isaf in Caernarvonshire, and Long-house and Burton in Pembrokeshire, which are either ruined Passage Graves or polygonal single chambers in the Passage Grave tradition.

Bryn Celli Ddu is in the east of Anglesey not many miles from the Menai Straits. It is a Passage Grave with a polygonal chamber set in a round barrow. It was excavated by W. J. Hemp in the years 1925 to 1929 and he noted a small incised

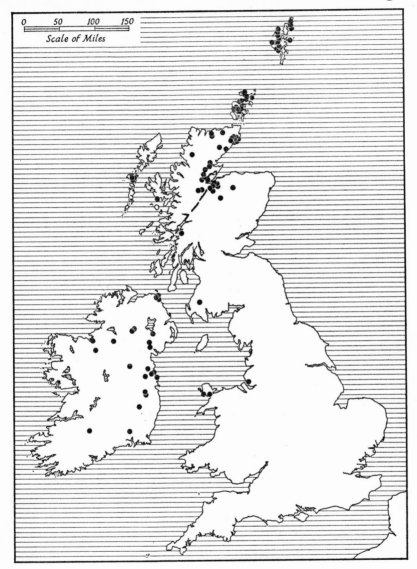

Fig. 28. Distribution map of Passage Graves in the British Isles

spiral on the inner face of one of the orthostats of the chamber. In the centre of the barrow and behind the chamber was a pit covered over by a megalith, and by its side another megalith which, lying prostrate in the centre of the mound, was decor-ated on part of its upper and under surfaces and on the edge between these surfaces, the decoration forming a continuous incised pattern. The pattern was made by linear pocking and consists of meandering lines, spirals, zigzags and a rectangle with zigzagged long sides.

Barclodiad y Gawres is some 12 miles west of Bryn Celli Ddu on a headland looking across to Ireland. It is a cruciform Passage Grave of Irish type set in a round mound. Excavations in 1952 and 1953 brought to light five decorated orthostats walling the passage and chambers. The motifs here were spirals, lozenges, horizontal bands or chevrons, and vertical zigzags as well as the possibility of an oculi or face motif on one of the stones (Stone 6). The most interesting stone at Barclodiad y

Plate 69

Gawres was Stone 22 with a design consisting of a central panel of two vertically arranged lozenges each with a double outline. On each side of these central lozenges are zigzag lines springing from the side edges of the orthostat. Above the central lozenges and flanking vertical zigzag lines is a band of horizon-tally-running chevrons. Above this the stone is badly weathered and has been damaged by stone-breakers but there was a much weathered spiral in the upper right-hand corner of the stone.

Many people will have heard of a suburb of Liverpool called the Calderstones; this took its name from a group of six stones that were until recently arranged in a circle and standing in a small fenced enclosure outside the Menlove Avenue en-trance to Calderstones Park. These stones were known as early as 1568 when they were referred to in a boundary dispute; they were then only three in number which presumably means that at that time only three stones were visible sticking out of a mound. The stones have now (1962) been removed to a storage depot in Liverpool preparatory to being set up in the Liverpool Museum. It is reasonable to assume that we have here the remains of a megalithic chambered tomb, perhaps a Passage Grave. All six stones are decorated and the motifs include single spirals, conjoined spirals, concentric circles, arcs, cup-marks, cup-and-ring marks, face and foot motifs. Perhaps the most interesting motifs are the two last-named. The face motifs occur on three of the stones and remind one at once of those on the underside of the capstone roofing the north side chamber at New Grange and at Knockmany. The foot motifs also occur on three stones and a total of ten representations occurs quite apart from the seven representations of boots cut in one of the stones in the nineteenth century. In addition to these motifs there are lozenges as at Barclodiad y Gawres and Fourknocks, and the representation of what—if it is an original design—is an Early Bronze Age halberd.

These three sites—Bryn Celli Ddu, Barclodiad y Gawres, and the Calderstones are the sum total of megalithic art on tombs in England and Wales. There is, however, a stone decorated with spirals in the style of Irish megalithic art in the church at Llanbedr in Merionethshire; it was found in the hills of Dyffryn Ardudwy and just possibly may be part of a vanished chambered tomb. There are curious engravings on the orthostats of the Ty Illtyd burial chamber in Brecknock-shire; they have often been claimed as prehistoric, and the Abbé Breuil compares them with engravings at Rathkenny and Clonfinloch in Ireland. But we take the view, held by many, that these engravings are not prehistoric and were added to the tomb at a later date.

There are, perhaps surprisingly, no Passage Graves in the Isle of Man. Scotland has Passage Graves in four separate areas, namely the south-west, the north-east, the Hebrides, and the Orkney–Cromarty region. The south-west sites include the White Cairn, Bargrennan, Minnigaff in Kirkcudbrightshire, and sites on Loch Etive such as Achnacree. In north-western Scotland there is a group of sites—some thirty or so of them—in the valleys of Strath Spey, the Nairn, Ness and Beauly, variously known as the Clava Group, the Beauly Group, and the Moray Group. This group has two kinds of tombs: first, typical Western European Passage Graves like Balnuaran or Clava West, Balnuaran or Clava East, and Avielochan; and secondly, closed circular chambers like Clava Middle, Daviot and Culdoich. In Skye and the Hebrides we find monuments in the Passage Grave tradition like Barpa Langass and Rudh'an Dunain. In the fourth area of Scottish Passage Graves, namely Caithness and the Orkneys, there are some remarkable ones like Maes Howe in the Orkneys and Camster in Caithness. These are in the full main tradition of West European Passage Grave architecture. Then there are also in the north of Scotland and in the Orkneys monuments in which the Passage Grave tradition of Camster and Maes Howe is varied and developed to produce curious monuments like Yarrows, Midhowe, Vinquoy and the Holm of Papa Westray.

Maes Howe on the mainland of Orkney is in its own way almost as remarkable a Passage Grave as New Grange. It is set in a round mound 115 feet in diameter and 24 feet high and consists of an entrance passage 36 feet long leading into a squared version of the cruciform plan. The central chamber is 15 feet square; the walls, made of dry walling, rise vertically for the first four and a half feet and then converge in overlapping courses. Maes Howe is partly destroyed, but the original structure still survives to a height of 12 feet 6 inches. Originally the dry-walled chamber with its corbelled vault must have been 18 to 20 feet high. The original top of the roof was removed when the site was excavated in 1861 but this was by no means the first time the tomb was broken into. It was broken into by the Vikings on their way to the Crusades in the twelfth century. The first visit is usually equated with the expedition of

Fig. 29. Distribution of sites with Passage Grave art in the British Isles

Earl Rognvald and Eindrid the Younger, which wintered in Orkney in 1150–1. Another visit to Maes Howe took place in January 1153 when Earl Harold and his men, who landed near Stromness, were in Maes Howe 'while a snow storm drove over them, and there two men of their band lost their wits, and that was a great hindrance to their journey.' These events are recorded in runic inscriptions on the walls of the tombs; the Vikings also made three engraved figures—a dragon, a walrus, and a serpent knot. Apart from these interesting twelfth-century inscriptions and figures Maes Howe has many remarkable structural features. The wall stones are beautifully shaped and dressed; there are four corner buttresses with the tops of the stones dressed diagonally away to key in with the overlapping corbels of the vault, and the side chambers, which are not on ground level but open several feet up in the side of the walls, have large blocking stones near by on the ground which could be used to close them completely. Indeed it is not surprising that the Royal Commission on the Ancient Monuments of Scotland should describe Maes Howe as 'the supreme example of its class in Great Britain'. Maes Howe and New Grange are certainly among the most splendid early pieces of architecture we have in the British Isles.

There are, in all these many and varied Passage Graves in Scotland, only two certain examples of megalithic art. The first of these is the big chambered cairn on the Holm of Papa Westray; this monument, which has been described by the Royal Commission on the Ancient Monuments of Scotland in their *Inventory of Monuments in Orkney* as 'one of the most interesting sepulchral structures in Orkney', has a series of engraved marks including in two places the oculi or eye motif. The second example is from a ruined cairn on Eday, a single stone now in the National Museum of Antiquaries of Scotland. It has engraved on it a pair of concentric circles and two conjoined spirals in a geometricized face motif.

The extraordinary face motif is found elsewhere in Britain in a non-megalithic context, namely on three decorated chalk cylinders (now in the British Museum) from a grave in a barrow on Folkton Wold in the East Riding of Yorkshire. These three chalk cylinders, often referred to as the 'Folkton drums', were found with the skeleton of a five-year-old child; they average 3½ inches high by 4 inches in diameter. The smallest of the three cylinders touched the child's head and the other two its hips. The motifs on these idols include not only the face, oculi or owl motif but also concentric circles within concentric-opposed horseshoes or spectacle marks, a four-pointed star, and filled-in lozenges and triangles—all designs in the repertory of megalithic art.

GRAVE GOODS

So far we have been concerned with the tombs themselves and their art. The grave goods dating from primary contexts found in the Irish Passage Graves consist of

(1) coarse *pottery* of a type usually referred to as Carrowkeel ware; it is decorated profusely with jabs, incisions, stab-and-drag marks. The pots were probably round-bottomed with massive flat-topped rims or simple thinned-out or externally bevelled rims. This pottery is also sometimes referred to as Loughcrew ware.

(2) *Pins and needles* of bone and antler, some of very large size —one from Carrowmore 15 is estimated to have been over 16 inches long, when intact. These pins have been classified by Piggott into three types which he calls mushroom-headed pins, poppy-headed pins, and skewer pins.

(3) *Stone beads and pendants*, the stone used being limestone, steatite, serpentine, jasper and carnelian. The commonest forms of beads are subconical barrel beads; there are also grooved globular beads and small ring or disc beads. Piggott has

divided the stone pendants into four types—pestle-shaped, rock-crystal drops, segmented, and triangular. There is also a single perforated tooth found in the Passage Grave on Belmore Mountain.

(4) *Stone and composition balls,* carefully made, with an average diameter of about 1 inch.

(5) *Stone axeheads*: a complete stone axehead was found at Baltinglass, and the chip of a polished flint axe from Lough-crew.

(6) *Flint arrowheads.* Loughcrew produced one leaf-shaped arrowhead and one barbed and tanged arrowhead.

In addition to this material, two examples of V-perforated stone buttons are known from Irish Passage Graves. These are of normal Western European type but it is uncertain as to whether they are part of the primary grave goods of the two tombs, namely Dowth and Carrowmore 49. Food-vessels have also been found in Irish Passage Graves but in most cases these seem to represent a subsequent re-use of the tombs by people of a different culture. Yet subsequent re-use might well have been continuous with the long initial primary use of a tomb. In Carrowkeel II a food-vessel of what would be described as the British Middle Bronze Age was found standing on the floor of a typical Cruciform Passage Grave, and must have been put there when access to the tomb in a normal primary way for funerary purposes was possible.

This may mean that while the grave goods are characteristic of pre-Food Vessel times in Ireland, the use of the tombs, and their importance and sanctity, carried through into Food-Vessel times, that is to say into the second half of the second millennium B.C. An analysis of the grave goods from the Irish Passage Graves—coarse pottery, bone pins and needles, stone beads, stone pendants, stone balls, axeheads and arrowheads—gives us without question a 'Neolithic' context if we use that phrase in a technological sense. There are no metal objects in primary contexts in the Irish Passage Graves. It does not give us an unequivocal or convincing context with the grave goods in the Breton and Iberian Passage Graves, to whom the builders of the Irish Passage Graves must have been related and must have kept in intermittent relationship. We find no *symbol-keramik* in the Irish tombs, no schist-plaques: nor any of the undecorated round-bottomed pottery—the so-called Western Neolithic ware—of Alcalá and Brittany.

THE ABBÉ BREUIL AND IRISH MEGALITHIC ART

In 1920 the late Abbé Henri Breuil visited Ireland in company with Professor R. A. S. Macalister and Mr M. C. Burkitt; he studied the megalithic art of the island and classified it into five groups. His conclusions were first set out in an article entitled 'Les Pétroglyphes d'Irlande' in the *Revue Archéologique* for 1921; then with Professor Macalister in a joint article in the *Proceedings of the Royal Irish Academy* for 1921-4, and at great length in his Presidential Address to the Prehistoric Society of East Anglia for 1934. The same classification and sequence was set out by Macalister on several occasions and by M. C. Burkitt in his *Prehistory* (1925) and *Our Early Ancestors* (1926). It has been widely accepted and, being the work of three distinguished archaeologists who have specialized in the study of early art, deserves our careful consideration, especially as we are unable to agree with those widely circulated views.

Breuil's first group, which he calls 'the oldest Decorative Art of Ireland', includes the incised patterns (crosses, circles, rectangles) on the Rathkenny burial chamber. The same incised engravings characterize his second group—the oldest of Breuil's four series of Passage Grave art; he includes here many patterns from Dowth (plain crosses, various circles and ovals containing a smaller circle), and only one design from New Grange, namely the faintly marked row of halved lozenges and triangles on stone C. 10, above the pocked triskele of spirals. Of these incised designs Breuil says roundly 'they are earlier than the other decorations on these monuments and appear to be pre
vious to their erection.'

His third group (the second in his Passage Grave series) is characterized by 'engravings picked in slender lines'. Breuil found many examples at Loughcrew (double triangles, anchor figures, circles, ovals, crosses, human faces), some at Dowth, and a great many at New Grange, particularly spirals and the human face. At Loughcrew he found some of the designs 'cer
tainly previous to the erection of the chief of the galleries contain
ing corbelled chambers' (one of his special examples was Cairn T), and at New Grange a great many of the designs 'certainly executed previous to the erection of that gigantic gallery of corbelled chambers.'

The fourth group (Breuil's Passage Grave Series Three) is characterized by 'engravings picked in wide and deep lines', and he divides it into two secondary groups as follows: *Group a*, an evolution of the preceding group in which the deep pocked lines were afterwards made regular by rubbing with a pebble, and *Group b*, consisting of curvilinear patterns sculptured in high relief. Breuil noted *Group a* at Loughcrew, Dowth, New Grange, Seskillgreen and Knockmany. *Group b* he found only at New Grange: it consists, according to him, of 'spirals in two or three scrolls . . . boxed arches, one in the other, oval cartouches with a double contour line containing deep cups separated from each other by triangular incisions'; in fact, this *group b* is no more and no less than the three kerb
stones a, b and c.

Breuil's fifth group (his Series Four of Passage Grave art) is characterized by engravings in rectilinear style: straight
line patterns existing only in lozenges and triangles often arranged in alternating groups. 'There is no doubt', said Breuil in his Presidential Address to the Prehistoric Society of East Anglia, 'as to the relatively late date of the straight-line patterns of New Grange.'

Here is then the Breuil–Macalister–Burkitt sequence of styles in Irish Passage Grave art: incised engravings, engravings picked in slender lines, engravings picked in wide and deep lines, sculptured high relief designs, and, finally, engraved triangles and lozenges. It is perfectly true, as we have already said, that there are many techniques used in the decorative art of New Grange and the other Irish Passage Graves. It is also true that some of the designs may antedate the construction of the Passage Graves, in New Grange as elsewhere. But is there any evidence for the sequence of these styles? May the sequence be no more than a well-intentioned and sincerely-felt academic exercise?

Mr T. G. E. Powell in his pioneer paper on 'The Passage Graves of Ireland' (*Proceedings of the Prehistoric Society*, 1938), was the first person to criticize seriously the Breuil sequence; 'in so far', he wrote, 'as this evolution is based on a faulty sequence of tomb types it seems likely that it will have ulti-mately to be revised.' The late Dr O. G. S. Crawford studied Irish megalithic art afresh in 1957 and in a tentative criticism of the Breuil sequence really demonstrated its complete absence of factual basis.

Crawford was prepared to agree that the sequence of styles was still 1, 2, 3a, but doubted whether 3b and 4 were later than the rest and said, 'When I say "later" I wish the word to be taken literally, as implying an interval of time that may be measured in minutes, hours or centuries.' He pointed out that some at least of the incised lines were made at the same time as the pricked ones, and 'possibly by the same person'; some, he thought, very rightly as we would think, 'were the artist's pre-liminary rough-out of the designs he was subsequently empha-sising in part by pricking.' Crawford goes on to say, 'I find it hard to believe that the Pricker and the Inciser belong to different cultures and periods or even that they were different persons.'

Crawford's criticisms were sound and fair but they did not go far enough. Mr Powell's suggestion that the sequence of styles is based on a faulty sequence of tomb types is only part of the trouble. We can find no evidence whatsoever of the sequence of styles set out by Breuil and approved by Macalister and Burkitt. The whole scheme, in our view, was based on faulty and hasty observation, and on the preconception that there ought to be a sequence of styles in megalithic art just as Breuil had argued there should be a sequence for Upper Palaeolithic cave art. The Breuil scheme of succeeding styles in Irish mega/ lithic art is, we think, a classic example of observer/imposed categories in archaeology.

MOTIFS IN THE ART

Fig. 30

While not agreeing with the Abbé Breuil's analysis of succes/ sive styles in Irish megalithic art, we agree with the broad lines of his classification of motifs in that art. This classification was developed later by Professor Piggott in his *The Neolithic Cul/ tures of the British Isles* (1954), and we reproduce here his analysis of the art motifs. His classification distinguishes twelve separate motifs and we now set this out in detail under his various headings:

(1) *Face/motifs.* The clearest form is 1c as seen on the underside of the capstone of the north side chamber at New Grange and on Knockmany. 1b which is a combination of spirals and lozenges, and 1a, a combination of multiple half/circles and half/ellipses, would appear to be, as Breuil first pointed out, distorted or derived or schematized versions of the face/motif so clear in 1c.

(2) *Circles.* These are commonly found and may be single (2a), multiple (2b), with a central dot (2c), or gapped (2d).

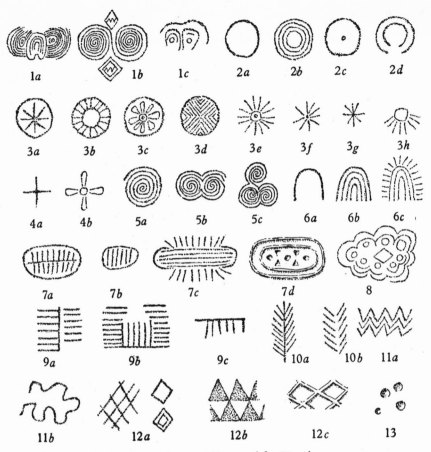

Fig. 30. Classification of motifs in Irish Passage Grave art (after Piggott)

(3) *Rayed Circles*. These can be single circles with rays or dots inside (3a), or double circles with rays in between (3b), circles with flower patterns inside (3c), circles with external rays (3e), a dot with external rays (3f), the asterisk symbol (3g), and the circle with an outer arc of rays (3h). Perhaps the most interesting motif in this group is what Piggott calls the 'circle with filled cross pattern' (3d). This is the motif that one finds on the tops of the circular-section marble idols of Iberia.

(4) *Crosses.* These are either simple crosses (4a) or developed petal-bladed crosses (4b).

(5) *Spirals*, as we have already seen, are well represented in Irish megalithic art and, as we shall see later, not so well repre-sented in megalithic art outside Ireland. We find the spirals set singly (5a), or in pairs, either running in the same direction (5b) or deliberately opposed as in Eday; and in one example only, in New Grange itself (Stone C10), the threefold or triskele arrangement (5c).

(6) *Arcs*, as they are called by Breuil and Piggott and more recently by Varagnac, but *half-ellipses*, as we would prefer to call them. These may be single (6a), multiple (6b) or rayed (6c). The multiple-rayed half-ellipse is often found in Irish megalithic art; in Brittany we find more often the single-rayed half-ellipse.

(7) *Ovals* or *ellipses* with transverse lines and lines on either side (7a, almost like a filleted fish), or with the vertical lines and no transverse lines (7b), or rayed and with a series of horizontal lines (7c), or with central relief carvings of triangles (7d).

(8) *Scalloped outlines.* This is the term given to them by Piggott. They are really assemblages of face motifs grouped together round a central lozenge.

(9) *Hurdle patterns.* These are horizontal lines in groups separ-ated or crossed by verticals in various combinations not readily susceptible to classification but including a sort of comb pat-tern (9c).

(10) These are the motifs described by the Abbé Breuil as *fir-tree motifs.* They consist of parallel rows of diagonal lines with (10a) or without (10b) a central line.

(11) *Zigzag patterns.* These are widespread in British megalithic art and may occur in angular form as a single line or generally as a parallel series of lines (11a). These are of course very well seen in New Grange, particularly on the lintel stones. The zigzag pattern is also seen in what Piggott called the 'rounded

or meander-like' form but which we prefer to call the zigzag leaf pattern (11b).

(12) *Triangles and lozenges,* which may be done in outline (12a), or be filled in by pecking (12b), or be in relief outline (12c) like the lintel stone over the entrance to New Grange.

(13) *Cup-marks* which occur commonly but never with an encircling ring. The cup-and-ring motif is found elsewhere in the British Isles and in Galicia.

Piggott's analysis of the Irish Passage Grave art motifs, and of course the analysis of the Abbé Breuil on which his was based, were published before the discovery of Fourknocks I and its excavation by Mr Hartnett, and also before the discovery of Barclodiad y Gawres in Anglesey. These two sites with their rich megalithic art mainly contain combinations of motifs already listed above. The exceptions are Barclodiad 7 and Stone *a* at Fourknocks, which in their combinations of circles and lozenges might suggest a figural representation. We think this is doubtful but, in any case, the motifs used in these com- binations are already present in Irish megalithic art and already listed above.

CHAPTER V

Cultural and Chronological Contexts

IN THIS FINAL CHAPTER we must consider the nature and significance of New Grange and the other tombs in the Bend of the Boyne, and answer the questions: By whom were these tombs set up? When? Why? Perhaps the least difficult question is the second. When we have determined the date of these tombs we can turn to the problem of the tomb-builders and their place in prehistoric Ireland. But the question of the date of the Boyne Passage Graves cannot be discussed apart from the whole problem of the date of Passage Graves in the British Isles and for that matter in Western Europe as a whole. In a recent note on New Grange (*Archaeological Journal*, 1960, 184), Dr Joseph Raftery, Keeper of Antiquities in the National Museum of Ireland wrote, 'An absolute date for New Grange has not been established but there is general agreement that it belongs to a period shortly before or shortly after 2000 B.C.' We must see whether we can agree with what is here described as general agreement.

There are two points that must be made at once: we can no longer speak of a date in the sense of a short period of years for the Passage Graves of the British Isles; we must in these days think of a long period of many centuries during which these tombs were constructed and used. Our task is, then, to find the maximum period during which Passage Graves were being built in the British Isles and then estimate when during this period the Boyne tombs were being built. Secondly, we must not necessarily suppose that the Boyne tombs are one-period constructions. Like Stonehenge or many a Christian cathedral these tombs may have been reconstructed, altered, rebuilt in various ways. This is particularly important in discussing the art. For example, the great stone at the entrance to New Grange has often and very rightly been compared with spirals at Mycenae such as those on the stelae from Shaft Grave 5 dis, covered by Schliemann. To accept this comparison and there, fore to date the stone at the entrance to, say, the fourteenth century B.C. is not to say that New Grange was built and first used in that century. The tomb itself could have been built in 3000 B.C. or 2500 B.C. or 2000 B.C., and have had a decorated stone in Mycenaean style added to it. Similarly, New Grange could have been built in 1000 B.C. or 500 B.C., and have in, corporated in its construction a decorated Mycenaean stone of the fourteenth century B.C.

Until a very few years ago the dating of prehistoric monu, ments in north,western Europe was done first, by setting them in the sequence of relatively dated technologies provided by the three,age system of Stone, Bronze and Iron; secondly, by attempting to give absolute dates to points in this relative sequence by the technique of cross,dating, that is to say, finding imports or exports that could be accurately dated in East Mediterranean and Near Eastern contexts. The application of these methods enabled archaeologists to refer to New Grange and the other Irish Passage Graves as 'late Neolithic' or 'early Bronze Age' and to make the sort of general date already quoted by Dr Raftery of 'shortly before or shortly after 2000 B.C.' In a study published in 1949 by one of us (G.E.D.) to, gether with Mr T. G. E. Powell we argued on these grounds of comparative archaeology and cross,dating that the bracket 1800 to 1200 B.C. was likely to encompass the chronological limits of the earliest and finest of the British Passage Graves, and in his chapter, 'Barbarian Europe' (*The Dawn of Civiliza, tion*, ed. Piggott, 1961), Powell writes of New Grange and the Boyne tombs that 'there are a number of reasons for believing these very large and skilfully built Passage Graves to date to the middle part of the second millennium B.C. and so to be largely contemporary with Mycenaean civilisation and the High Bronze Age of Middle Europe.'

In 1946 Professor Willard F. Libby discovered the technique of Carbon 14 dating and in the last few years various radio-carbon laboratories have determined dates in absolute years for Passage Graves and associated monuments which enable us to dispense with the laborious and often uncertain techniques of cross-dating. Some of the dates obtained by C 14 analysis differ considerably from those current in text-books and general archaeological writing before the appearance of this geochrono-logical technique, but it should be remembered very clearly that many of the pre-C 14 dates were largely the result of guesswork. Gordon Childe used to say that there was no certain date in the prehistory of north-western Europe before the trade in faience beads of the period 1600–1400 B.C. The absolute dates quoted before this period were estimations. There was in the last fifteen years a general consensus of opinion that the Neolithic 'period' began between 2500 and 2000 B.C. Now it is clear that the Neolithic began in north-western Europe around 3500 B.C. As many megalithic tombs are obviously Neolithic and few contain metal objects (although they may have been and indeed many were constructed in a Bronze Age context), it follows that some tombs could be dated into the second half of the fourth millennium B.C.

And from megalithic monuments in Brittany come C 14 determinations of this period. The Passage Grave in the Sept-Iles archipelago, off Perros-Guirec in the Côtes-du-Nord which yielded western Neolithic pottery, contained some twig charcoal giving dates of 3055 ± 150 B.C., 3215 ± 130 B.C., and 3450 ± 135 B.C. The Passage Grave on Ile Carn, Ploudal-mezeau, Finistère gave a C 14 date of 3030 ± 60 B.C. The megalithic Passage Grave of Kercado, Carnac gave an even earlier date, namely 3880 ± 300 B.C. Unless we are prepared to discount these dates—and there is no good reason why we should—it is now clear that some Passage Graves were being built in north-western Europe in the second half of the fourth millennium B.C.

We also know from C14 dating that Passage Graves were being built a thousand years later, namely in the second half of the third millennium B.C. The Passage Grave of Mané-Kernaplaye, Saint-Philibert, Morbihan gave C14 dates of 2470 ± 120 and 2785 ± 120 B.C. Direct and interesting evidence comes from Ireland itself, namely from the Mound of the Hostages at Tara. The excavation of this site was begun by one of us (S.P.ÓR.) and completed by Professor R. de Valera. It is a small Passage Grave with one stone decorated in the style of the Boyne art, and primary archaeological material typical of the Boyne Passage Graves. Under the mound was a ditch; charcoal from the filling of this ditch gave a date of 2120 ± 160 B.C. The ground on which the mound was constructed had been burnt prior to construction; the remains of the burning were represented by a black smear over much of the ground surface. This smear consisted of charcoal and carbonized seeds and gave a C 14 date of 2300 ± 160 B.C. Close to the entrance to the passage a large fire had been lit on the old ground surface which Professor de Valera considered contemporary with or at most very slightly later than the building of the barrow. Charcoal from this fire gave a date of 1920 ± 150 B.C. It is therefore fairly certain that the Passage Grave of the Mound of the Hostages was built about 2100 B.C.

Evidence from the Isles of Scilly and from the *causses* country of south Central France suggests that some megalithic tombs were being constructed and used as late as the end of the second millennium B.C. The evidence available to us at present then suggests that in some parts of Western Europe megalithic tombs were being built from 3500 to 1000 B.C., i.e. for two and a half thousand years. This is quite a new concept; most of the archaeological text-books of ten years ago and more would only give megalithic architecture a duration of two or three centuries, or at most half a millennium. Yet now we must get used to the idea that some kinds of megaliths were being constructed in Europe from the fourth to the first millennia B.C.

Two archaeologists have argued that they were being built and used at a much more recent date than is suggested here. One of these was the late Miss V. C. C. Collum, whose excavations at the Tressé Gallery Grave south of St Malo in Ille-et-Vilaine and at the Déhus monument on Guernsey convinced her, but very few other people, that these megalithic tombs were built in Gallo-Roman times. The other is Dr Joseph Raftery, whose views on the date of New Grange we have already quoted. Dr Raftery's views on the lateness of some Passage Graves is based on his re-excavation of Carn H at Loughcrew, and as this tomb is closely allied in plan to New Grange, and is in any case one of the Irish Passage Graves, we must consider his arguments carefully.

In his original excavations at Loughcrew H, Conwell found bone pins, fragments of the pottery which Childe called Carrowkeel ware, flints, sea-shells and stone balls (six underneath the stone basin in the northern chamber). In the southern chamber and its entrance Conwell found a remarkable collection of bone implements, glass, amber, bronze and iron. The bone implements were mainly plaques: Conwell saved 4,071 fragments of them, and Raftery estimated that there were 3,000 complete plaques of which 100 were ornamented with circles and curvilinear designs. These bone plaques or objects—whatever we like to call them—are 10 to 15 centimetres long, 2 to 3 centimetres wide and have a pointed and a half-rounded end. They are slightly convex to the middle and have sharp edges. Raftery describes them as 'very much like modern paper knives'. The amber objects were seven beads; the glass objects included three small beads, the iron objects iron rings, a piece of a knife and the leg of a compass with which Conwell thought the circular designs had been made, and an iron punch which Conwell thought had been used for punching or pick-ing out the designs.

The ornament on these bone plaques is by very general con-sent agreed to belong to La Tène art and probably to date to the first two centuries A.D. The problem presented by these objects of La Tène art together with iron objects was to explain their presence in a Passage Grave the walls of which were decorated with typical megalithic art and which was assumed by most people to have been constructed in or around 2000 B.C. It was argued by most archaeologists before Dr Raftery's re-excavations that Carn H at Loughcrew had been used as a workshop in the Early Iron Age—perhaps the *atelier* of a Celtic artist. Professor Macalister, for example, believed that metal-workers of the Early Iron Age produced these bone plaques as samples for the ornamentation of luxury objects of bronze. Dr Raftery disagreed with this view and in 1943 re-excavated Carn H.

The 1943 Raftery excavations found no objects characteris-tic of the normal megalithic assemblage: what was found, however, were blue, green and yellow glass beads, small bronze rings, pieces of iron and 2,000 bone plaques of which 200 were ornamented in the late La Tène style. Raftery argued that all these finds dated to the Early Iron Age; he found some of them in what he described as an undisturbed foundation layer, while some bone plaques were actually in the stone-hole of one of the orthostats in the passage. In describing his excavations to the International Congress of Prehistoric and Protohistoric Sciences at Zürich in 1954, he thought the evidence in his excavations susceptible of only two solutions: first, that the site was a normal Passage Grave constructed, say, in 2000 B.C. but entirely destroyed, removed and rebuilt in the Early Iron

Age; or secondly, that it was an old style of tomb still being used in the Early Iron Age. Having found no evidence for the first solution, he has put it on record that Carn H was con⁄ structed in the Early Iron Age and that therefore megaliths in Ireland survived not only to the end of the second millen⁄ nium B.C. but *to the beginning of the first millennium A.D.*

These are surprising and astonishing conclusions but so to most people are the radiocarbon dates that put the construction of some Passage Graves at 3500 B.C. If we are to reframe our ideas of megalithic chronology to allow tombs fifteen hundred years before the generally accepted date of about 2000 B.C., there is no reason why we should not reframe them to allow tombs fifteen hundred or two thousand years after the generally accepted date *provided the evidence warrants this conclusion.* We are not, however, convinced that the evidence from Loughcrew H does so warrant it. Dr Raftery's interpretation does not take into consideration the art on the walls of this tomb. This is normal megalithic art such as occurs in other tombs in this cemetery and elsewhere. No evidence known to us suggests that this art can be dated anywhere in Europe after 1500 B.C. and we find it inconceivable that one group of people living in the second century A.D. should have practised two quite separate forms of art—La Tène art on their bone plaques, and yet on the walls of their tomb pecked designs in a quite different style extinct in Europe for over a thousand years. The answer to the Carn H riddle must lie in disturbance, reconstruction and re⁄use although the excavator did not find traces of this.

We do not, then, regard Carn H as showing that Passage Grave building or megalithic art survived in Ireland until the Roman conquest of Britain. The range of such tomb building in north⁄western Europe would appear to be from 3500 B.C. to 1000 B.C. Where in this very wide period of two and a half millennia should we place the Irish Passage Graves and especi⁄ ally New Grange and Dowth?

We have four separate pieces of evidence to help us answer this question. The first is the Carbon 14 date for the Mound of the Hostages to which reference has already been made. The second is the archaeological evidence of the secondary use of the Irish Passage Graves. The third is the comparative study of the art on the walls and roofs of the tombs, and the fourth is the comparative study of the morphology of the tombs.

We have said that it seems reasonable to suppose that the Passage Grave in the Mound of the Hostages at Tara was con/ structed about 2100 B.C. It has on one of its walling stones art characteristic of the great Boyne tombs. If any theory of the typology of Passage Graves carries any weight, the V/shaped Passage Graves come late in a series beginning with circular or polygonal tombs, and are intermediate between the early tombs and the Entrance Graves of the Scilly/Tramore Group. The Mound of the Hostages site is a V/shaped Passage Grave. The evidence from this site alone would suggest that at least some of the Irish Passage Graves were built before 2100 B.C.

The secondary material in the Irish Passage Graves is Food Vessel material and this was again clearly demonstrated in the Tara excavations. The primary assemblage of grave goods in the Passage Graves, namely round/bottomed Carrowkeel/style pottery, hammer/pendants, stone and composition balls, large mushroom/ and poppy/headed pins, dates from before any Food Vessel horizon; yet the contemporaneity of some of this material with the Wessex Early Bronze Age culture of southern Britain, covering the period from 1700 to 1400 B.C., cannot be denied. A secondary burial later than the main Passage Grave in the Mound of the Hostages contained faience beads, and at Harristown in County Waterford a quoit/shaped bead of glassy faience was found with a bone pin with perforated head and a notched/base bronze knife in a cordoned urn in a cremation cemetery secondary to the V/shaped Passage Grave or Entrance Grave which was the primary burial in the mound.

The comparative study of the mural megalithic art of the Irish and British Passage Graves may be approached by analysing the three main motifs represented. There are, first, the geometrical patterns excluding the spiral, that is to say the zigzags, chevrons, lozenges and triangles. Secondly, there are the face motifs such as occur on the capstone of the north side chamber at New Grange, at Knockmany, on the Holm of Papa Westray, and on the Folkton idols. In the third place there are the spirals. Let us consider these motifs separately.

The geometrical patterns without any doubt find their closest and indeed very close parallels in the art of the collective tombs of Iberia. This art appears in two forms: murally, when it is painted and engraved on the walls of tombs mainly in northern Portugal and north-western Spain; and in mobiliary form, when it occurs on decorated idols and plaques and on pots in the tombs of southern Portugal and southern Spain. The vertical zigzag patterns are well seen in the Pedralta (Cota) and Pedra Coberta (Jallas) tombs in north Portugal but these geometrical patterns as a whole are best paralleled on the decorated schist plaques which occur so frequently in south Portuguese tombs. In 1937 the late Dr Adolf Mahr said, 'I frequently wondered why nobody ever troubled to say in plain words that the famous kerb-stone *b* at New Grange or the stone outside the east recess of this monument show exactly the same pattern as the anthropomorphic Portuguese schist idols.' This is what much of Irish mural Passage Grave art is—the translation into mural form of the patterns of south Iberian mobiliary megalithic art. This south Iberian art is itself rooted in the early artistic traditions of the East Mediterranean and is particularly well seen in the flat idols of red polished ware of rectangular shape found from the Early Bronze Age in Cyprus and dated to between 2300 and 2100 B.C.

The face motif (or oculi motif, or the representation of the Earth-Mother Goddess or Funerary Deity) is well known in northern France. It occurs on the underside of the capstone of the great Déhus monument from Guernsey, and in several examples of the rock-cut and surface collective tombs in the Paris Basin. In Brittany, as in some of the Paris Basin tombs, we find a concentration on some features of the goddess other than the eyes and face, namely the necklace or the breasts, and in some Breton tombs we have nothing except the repetition of pairs of breasts. It is clear that in Brittany as in the British Isles we are dealing with a formalized iconography of a goddess figure in which certain parts—eyes or breasts—have assumed the visual role of the complete figure seen elsewhere.

In the north of Spain a figure in many ways like the Déhus goddess comes from the Dolmen de Corao, Abamia in Asturias, and in the province of Huelva there is a very good representation of the goddess—eyebrows, nose and breasts—on the walls of the Dolmen de Soto. But the most common representations of this cult figure in southern Iberia is again in the mobiliary art of the tombs. The stylized face motif is well seen on many of the Portuguese schist plaques, in the marble and limestone cylinders and decorated phalange bones of southern Spain and perhaps best of all on some of the pots from the collective chamber tombs. A fine pot from Los Millares 7 (now in the Ashmolean Museum, Oxford), with its eyes and eyebrows, is an excellent example of what Georg and Vera Leisner have called *symbolkeramik*—pottery bearing in symbolic form the representation of the eye-goddess.

In the South of France and particularly in the departments of the Aveyron, Tarn, Gard, and Bouches-du-Rhône there have been found some fifty sculptured menhirs usually referred to as statues-menhirs which delineate the Mother-Goddess. Only two or three of them are connected with chamber tombs, and none of them can be accurately dated. They must, however, represent some aspect of the Funerary Goddess cult seen in the tombs of Iberia and northern France. At Peña Tu, between

Santander and Llanes (Asturias) in north Spain there is on a natural rock-surface a painted and engraved version of this goddess-figure which is something in between the figures on the tombs of Abamia and De Soto and the free-standing statue-menhirs of southern France. There are other smaller figures on this rock-surface and the representation of a metal dagger of the Early Bronze Age. There is no proof that the painted and engraved figure is contemporary with the dagger, but if it were, it might imply some date early in the second millennium B.C.

In Sardinia small stylized figures of goddesses have been found, one of which, from Senorbi, is remarkably like the Cycladic idol figures. In northern Italy and in the last few years in Corsica statues-menhirs have been found that are much later in date than the tombs and menhirs in France and Spain that we have been discussing, and may indicate a survival of this cult figure into the Late Bronze Age.

The great megalithic monuments of Malta have yielded the head of a statue-menhir from tomb 5 at Zebbuġ and many representations of a goddess-figure (or at least an obese female), which most archaeologists think are derived from Cycladic sculpture. A C 14 date of 2690 ± 150 B.C. from Mġarr in Malta suggests that the statue-menhir and some of the other figures may date from the first half of the third millennium.

We have already mentioned Cycladic figurines. Here from the Early Bronze Age, early in the third millennium B.C., are stylized female figurines some of which have inspired the cult art of the West Mediterranean and Western Europe. From Troy I come a heart-shaped face on stone and many face-designs on pottery, and from Tell Brak in the Khabur valley of eastern Syria many eye-idols found in what Professor Max Mallowan, the excavator of the site, has called the Eye Temple. Here in Syria and in the representations of Troy and the Cyclades we have perhaps a context and a date for the begin-ning of this goddess cult which spread up to France and the

British Isles. Professor Mallowan would date the Eye Temple at Brak to about 3000 B.C. The date of Troy I is still a matter of discussion but in a fresh analysis of its chronology in the light of C 14 dates Mr James Mellaart has suggested that Troy I may begin as early as *c.* 3500 B.C.

We need go no further in this discussion than to emphasize that there is a reasonably dated context of the second half of the fourth millennium for the eye-goddess motif in the East Mediterranean. We are now left with the third of the motifs we isolated in Irish megalithic art, namely the spiral, and we have already commented that this only occurs rarely. It appears even more rarely in the megalithic art of France and Iberia than in the British Isles. Spirals occur at Gavrinis in Brittany, but we know of no examples of spirals in an Iberian megalithic tomb. There are, however, spirals on a slab from Monte de Eiro, Marco de Canavases in Portugal, and here they are part of a design which includes leaf-shaped patterns in much the same way as does the pattern stone at Bryn Celli Ddu. Spirals are very common in the megalithic art of Malta, and if we accept the C 14 date from Mgarr and the revised chronology of Professor Bernabò Brea for these sites, the Maltese spirals would date from the third millennium B.C.

Many archaeologists, from Coffey onwards, have argued that the Irish spirals are inspired by Mycenaean art and made the comparison, to which we have already referred, between the entrance slab at New Grange, for example, and the decorated stelae from Shaft Grave 5 at Mycenae. Another comparison is with the decorated blocking slabs at Castelluccio in Sicily, which Brea would date on synchronisms with the more evolved phases of the Middle Helladic and the beginning of the Late Helladic phases in Greece as approximately between 1800 and 1400 B.C. It has been suggested that the spiral is an added element in the art of the British megaliths, that while the body of the art belonged to an earlier tradition of the third millennium

Plate 70

with its geometrical patterns and eye-motifs, the spiral is a fresh element of Mycenaean times.

For a while we were impressed by these arguments, but it seems to us that it is not really possible to disentangle the spiral from associated zigzag and chevron patterns in the decorated tombs of Ireland and Wales. The art appears to us to be a unity. We are much impressed by Bernabò Brea's verdict (*Antiquity*, 1960, 135) that 'the great Megalithic culture of Malta had already disappeared by 1650 B.C. . . . it is impossible to see in it the reflections of the Mycenaean civilisation.' Similarly the art in the Boyne tombs appears to us not in any way to be a reflection of Mycenaean civilization but of the pre-Mycenaean civilization that flourished in the Cyclades, Troy, Crete, Malta and Iberia in the third millennium B.C. In the art alone there is a powerful argument for reinforcing the deductions to be made from the C 14 dates of the Mound of the Hostages at Tara.

We must now turn to the fourth piece of evidence we listed as likely to assist us in trying to date the Boyne tombs, namely the form of the tombs themselves. Megalithic Passage Graves like Bryn Celli Ddu can be best paralleled in Brittany and in Portugal. The cruciform Passage Grave like New Grange and Barclodiad y Gawres has its best parallel in southern Spain and Portugal. There is no exact parallel to the symmetrical Cruciform Passage Grave in southern Iberia, but in the great cemetery of Los Millares and the smaller cemetery of Alcalá in south Portugal there are tombs with side chambers that could have given rise to the Irish cruciform type. We must, then, try to know the date of these Iberian monuments.

Many different views have been held as to the origin, affinities and dates of the Iberian collective tombs. It has been suggested, for example, that small megalithic tombs originated in northern Portugal and Galicia in a 'Neolithic' context, and spread southwards developing first into megalithic Passage

Graves and then into dry-walled and corbel-roofed tombs of the type found at Los Millares and Alcalá, and the rock-cut tombs such as those of Palmella and Alapraia near Lisbon. By the time these developments took place the culture of the tomb-builders was in the Eneolithic or Copper Age. This view does not take into account the very close parallels between the art of the Iberian tombs and the early art of the East Mediter-ranean which we have just discussed; to most people the art (both the geometrical motifs and the eye-goddess motifs) was introduced into Iberia from the East Mediterranean by the builders of the dry-walled and rock-cut collective tombs.

Recently Dr Beatrice Blance studied the Early Bronze or Copper Age sites in Iberia representing the introduction into Iberia of the people responsible for the collective tombs and the religious art. She referred to these sites as colonies, not only because it was the word used by Siret (though admittedly he thought that Los Millares was a Phoenician colony!) but also because Georg and Vera Leisner use the term *Factorei*. She listed six such colonies for certain, and they are shown on the map. Three are known only by settlements, namely Carmona, Mesas de Asta and Vila Nova de Sao Pedro, one—Alcalá— *Fig. 31* only by a cemetery of tombs, and two—Los Millares and Almizaraque—by cemeteries and settlements. The dating of these settlements which are surely ancestral to the Irish Passage Graves is a key issue in the chronology of Passage Graves in Western Europe as a whole.

So far only one C 14 date is known from these settlements. A sample of carbon, found below the tumble of the settlement wall at Los Millares gave a date of 2345 ± 85 B.C. The initial settlement of Los Millares must, then, be well before this. Dr Blance made a special study of parallels between the Iberian colonies and the presumed home settlements in the Eastern Mediterranean and concluded that the earliest Iberian settle-ments were between 2700 and 2600 B.C. Two considerations should be borne in mind here: the quoted date for Los Millares should now be adjusted in the light of various modifi-cations in C 14 dating which have taken place in the last few years; secondly, if Mr Mellaart's arguments for a much earlier chronology for Troy I are accepted, Dr Blance's parallels date from before 2700 B.C. The C 14 date for Los Millares would now appear to be 2500 B.C. and this is by no means a date for the commencement of the Millaran colony. If Troy I may have begun at 3500 B.C., the parallels between, say, the pottery at Mesas de Asta and Tigani in Samos suggest a date as early as this for some of the Iberian colonies.

It therefore seems most likely to us at the moment that the early colonies in Iberia were established between 3500 and 2700 B.C. At the moment and until we have a large number of C 14 dates from Iberian collective tombs we cannot refine these dates. The sum total of our discussion in the last few pages is this: we know from direct evidence that some of the Irish Passage Graves were built before 2100 B.C., whilst the com-parative evidence from Iberia as well as from Brittany suggests that the first Irish Passage Graves could have been built be-tween 3500 and 3000 B.C. Our own view, put forward tenta-tively, is that the half-millennium between 3000 and 2500 B.C. saw the beginning of the building of Passage Graves in Ireland, the practice continuing until the first half of the second millen-nium. There is no direct evidence as yet for putting New Grange at any particular point in the series and it is only guess-work when we suggest that it might have been built at 2500 B.C. ± 250 years. We realize that this is much earlier than both of us have argued on several occasions before when a date between 1900 and 1600 seemed probable; but these views were based on two premises, the late dating of the Neolithic and Copper Age in the Mediterranean, and an insistence on Mycenaean and Wessex parallels. We now accept Brea's arguments that the great floruit of megalithic culture in Malta and in Western Europe was before Mycenaean times; the arguments from C 14 dates for a much earlier chronology for the Neolithic in the Mediterranean and Western Europe are surely inescapable. We realize that there is no direct evidence for the date of New Grange itself, and that C 14 determinations at the site may at any moment prove us quite wrong. It is after all only one—albeit the finest—of the Irish Passage Graves; the inescapable conclusion at present seems to us that the Irish Passage Graves are mainly the work of the third millennium B.C.

Can we now answer the question: Who built New Grange? The answer is a simple one. It was the people who spread from Spain and Portugal to Brittany on the one hand and to Ire/land on the other. The builders of the tombs in the Bend of the Boyne were colonists from Iberia, and somewhere in eastern Ireland as in north Wales and the Morbihan we should be able to locate settlements like Mesas de Asta, Carmona and Vila Nova de Sao Pedro. The special peculiarity of Vila Nova de Sao Pedro and Los Millares is the buttressed construction of the walls; similar semicircular bastions have recently been found by Dr Jean Arnal at a site called Lébous in the Hérault of southern France in an area full of Passage Graves. Perhaps a site with semicircular bastions waits discovery in Ireland; such a settlement site would put our knowledge of the Passage Grave builders on a very firm foundation.

The time has now come to attempt an interpretation in his/torical terms of the archaeological evidence we have been dis/cussing in this chapter and the archaeological description of a group of tombs in the Boyne valley to which this book is devoted. We suggest that in the early third millennium B.C., and perhaps even well before 3000 B.C., groups of people from the East Mediterranean set out by ship to the Middle and West Mediterranean looking for new places to live and perhaps also for some of the sources of the raw materials (such as copper) used by them in their homeland. These people made landfalls in Iberia and among their early settlements are Los Millares, Almizaraque, the Cadiz area, the south of Portugal and the Tagus estuary. Some of their settlements were fortified enclósures with semicircular bastions; they were farmers using stone tools and copper tools. They buried their dead in large tombs built with dry stone walls and roofed with a corbelled vault, and in tombs cut in the soft rock. The plan of these tombs was circular, sometimes with a short passage but often with a long passage and so producing the plan referred to as a Passage Grave. They were communal tombs used collectively by a family or neighbourhood group. These early colonists in Iberia brought some pottery and grave goods with them from their homelands, but also used in Spain and Portugal the artifacts of the préexisting Neolithic people whom they met and mixed with. They brought with them a religion in which the main figure seems to have been an Earth Mother or Funeŕary Goddess and the representation of this cult figure appears on pots, on portable idols and on the walls of their tombs.

Some of these Iberian colonists moved on to Brittany, the west coast of France and Normandy and up the English Channel to Denmark and north́west Germany where there is some evidence of their arrival by 2700 B.C. They also crossed the sea from Brittany or Spain to Ireland and settled there. New Grange and the tombs in the Bend of the Boyne are, then, the tombs of these settlers, who spread up from Ireland and Wales to Scotland and the Orkneys. The great tomb of Maes Howe in Orkney, almost as great an architectural monument as New Grange itself, is particularly interesting in that its side chambers are not placed at ground level as at New Grange but up in the sides of the walls—a feature exactly paralleled at Alcalá in south Portugal.

We must not imagine these colonial voyages to be single journeys of exploration. The contacts to which we refer may

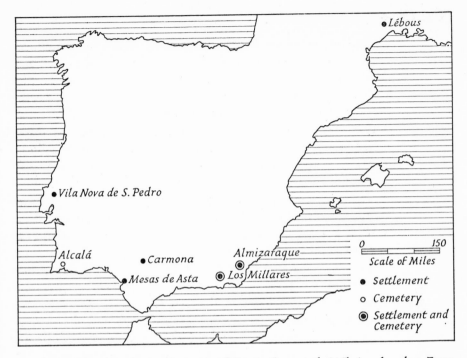

Fig. 31. Map of settlement sites and cemeteries of Passage Grave people in Iberia and southern France (after Blance)

have taken place over many centuries, and we may be certain that the colonies kept in touch with other colonies and perhaps even with the mainland. The resemblances between the art of New Grange and that of Gavrinis must be due to cousinly connections. The contacts between Mycenae and Wessex and Ireland which developed in the second millennium may well be a continuation of the relationships set up a thousand years before. We can do no more than speculate on the sort of ships which these early people used; the engraving at New Grange called 'Coffey's ship', even if it is a ship, is no help to us. The Scandinavian Bronze Age rock engravings of ships do show us vessels that might have been used further back in the third millennium. These people probably used skin boats such as those that survive as the umiak among the Eskimo and the curragh in Ireland, or even wooden boats that survive on the western coasts of Portugal and Spain as the saveiro—boats, incidentally, which bear on their prows eye or oculus ornament that may go back to the third millennium. Whatever ships they used, our admiration goes out to these pioneer sailors. Many of them must have been lost as they journeyed and trafficked along the Atlantic seaways, exploring routes and tides and conditions that were to be used later by Phoenicians and Greeks. These megalithic men were doing in 3000 B.C. what Pytheas the Greek navigator and mathematician did in 325 B.C. or thereabouts.

They penetrated from the Mediterranean to Ireland, the Orkneys and Jutland, and there is no more moving testimony of their ancient prowess than to see in the Copenhagen National Museum pots from Passage Graves with the ancient oculi patterns like those on the *symbolkeramik* of southern Iberia or to look at the scribings on the tomb on the Holm of Papa Westray in Orkney or the slab from Eday now in the National Museum of Antiquities of Scotland and see the ghostly end of Mediterranean megalithic art in Ultima Thule. Did these megalithic seafarers get any further? Some of them must have got to the Canary Islands because here, not on tombs but on rock surfaces, there are remarkable examples of what we have been calling megalithic art. Indeed it has been one of our favourite tricks to show photographs of some of the Canary Islands art to professional archaeologists and students not already aware of it and to ask where it comes from. The invariable answer is that it is a slab from one of the lesser known tombs at Loughcrew.

Did any of these intrepid seamen get across the Atlantic? In Connecticut, at North Salem, there are some strange remains that are always being brought to the attention of European specialists in megalithic architecture. They have been especially studied by Mr Frank Glynn, President of the Con-necticut Archaeological Society, and are now managed and run as a tourist attraction by a small syndicate. They are called Mystery Hill; but there is no mystery. They are a folly built by a Mr Jonathan Pattee in the eighteenth century and are no more a genuine megalithic monument than the Margate Grotto is a Phoenician shrine. We mention Mystery Hill, North Salem especially because in a recent book, *Land to the West*, its author, Geoffrey Ashe is swept away by the claims of the site to be a North American megalith. One would think that the plan alone, with its grooved sacrificial table, stone bed, altar, speaking tube, and drains, was enough to show we are not dealing with a prehistoric megalith. There is no reason why the megalith builders who voyaged from Almeria and Anda-lucia to County Meath and Sjaelland might not have made perhaps one successful voyage across the Atlantic, or perhaps a voyage that came to grief as the result of a storm. We must always remember the ten Japanese castaways who in 1915 were blown off the coast of Japan and drifted for fifty days across the north Pacific in their small dismasted schooner, subsisting on very little food and rain-water before being picked up off the coast of British Columbia; or the three Japanese who in 1845 were blown or had drifted in a little junk across the Pacific to Mexico. The megalith builders could have sailed, or been blown, or drifted across the Atlantic. We have no evidence, however, that this happened, and 'the megalith builders of America' is one of the many myths which the un-reasoning mind of those who dwell on the lunatic fringes of archaeology like to encourage.

But the Passage Grave Builders of Ireland fascinate us no less because they cannot be shown to have crossed the Atlantic. What was the state of culture of these seafarers and why did they come to Ireland? The first question is posed in old text-

Plate 14

books in the form: were they Neolithic or Bronze Age? We know that no metal objects have been found in primary association in any Irish Passage Grave; we also know that on Stone R. 18 in the passage at New Grange are marks made by a metal chisel. We know too that if the Irish Passage Graves are derived from the collective tombs of southern Iberia, if they represent colonies from places like Los Millares and Alcalá, then at least in their homelands these colonists must have understood well the use of copper. Of course these labels Neolithic, Copper Age and Bronze Age derive from a time when the prehistoric past of man was conceived of in unitary and geological terms.

For a long time people tended to regard prehistory as rather like a chestofdrawers and the responsibility of the archaeologist was thought to have ceased when he had pigeonholed his material by putting it in the right drawer or hole. This analogy is now invalidated, for we know two things which upset the simple unitary, one chestofdrawers sequence. The first is that people could have known the use of metal in one country but not in a neighbouring one; that is to say that the Bronze Age in one country, or at least the beginning of the Bronze Age, could have been contemporary with the end of the Neolithic in a neighbouring country. The second is that the sequence of Neolithic, Bronze Age, and Iron Age is an idealistic one based on the supposed natural material progress of man, and the observed technological progress in many countries. What it did not allow for—and this is quite understandable as it was developed at a time when nineteenthcentury ideas of progress were common—is the possibility of retrogression as well as progression. The loss of useful arts is well attested among modern primitive peoples where craftsmen may die out or a move may be made to an environment where basic materials are no longer available. Thus the absence of pottery in Polynesia is often attributed to a lack of suitable clay in the islands, or to the presence of easily obtained substitutes such as coconut shells. The whalebone net, a characteristic feature of Eskimo culture, is missing from the Hudson Bay region because of the lack of the raw material.

The colonists of southern Iberia were metal-users as they had been in their East Mediterranean homeland. It is inconceivable that those of them who set out on further journeys to the north from Los Millares and Alcalá were not still aware of the making of copper tools; indeed it may well be that one of the reasons for their journeys to western France and the British Isles was to find sources of copper. The Passage Graves of the Hérault in southern France almost certainly represent the tombs of metal prospectors from southern Spain and so does the settlement of Lébous belong to metal-using folk although it may well date from much later than the south Spanish sites.

We can therefore say that the builders of the earliest Irish Passage Graves belonged to a society, or came from a society, that understood the working of metal. Why, then, is there no metal in their tombs? There are two possible reasons: one is that they did not find the sources of copper for which they were looking; a second is that even if they did, and exploited the copper, they would have sent it back to their Iberian homelands and not buried tools made from it in their own tombs. We should perhaps think of the whole problem in this way: here are colonists looking for land and metal. Land is easy to find but copper ores not so easy; there were no geological maps and there was no knowledge of metallurgy among the indigenous inhabitants of Ireland whom they met—the Neolithic peasant farming societies first established in Ireland and Britain in the middle of the fourth millennium B.C. These contacts were perhaps being made in the first half of the third millennium B.C. The culture of the colonists which came into existence in the first half of the third millennium was not formally Neolithic in its Iberian homeland, nor Neolithic in intention in Ireland. The culture of the builders of New Grange and elsewhere is therefore Chalcolithic or Copper Age. That they certainly knew the use of metal is shown by Stone R. 18 at New Grange, and it would be a very bold archaeologist who categorically denied the possibility that the axes on one of the decorated stones at Gavrinis were not representations of copper axeheads. Then there may be a psycho-sociological factor involved. It might have been that in the lives of these Iberian colonists in Ireland and Brittany metal was rare and so highly prized that they did not wish to put metal objects in their tombs. Indeed, in Brittany the only explanation of some of the remarkable jadeite and chloromelanite axeheads buried in megalithic tombs is that they were copies of metal axes; perhaps because metal was so rare and the old material used for axeheads was stone, it was thought appropriate that such stone representations of metal axes should be buried.

Whatever is the correct explanation, it means that the labels Neolithic, Chalcolithic, and Bronze Age cannot be used in any sensible and modern meaningful use with regard to New Grange. When settlements of the Boyne tomb builders have been found and excavated we shall be in a better position to talk about their technology. But it seems fair to say even at this moment that New Grange and the other tombs in the Bend of the Boyne are the tombs of people living in Ireland in the third millennium who knew the use of metal—at least had knowledge of the smelting and casting of copper tools, but were not bronzesmiths.

Ireland developed as one of the great centres of metal-working in the Bronze Age properly so called; this was in the early second millennium B.C. It may well be that the original societies of the Boyne people survived to become those who initiated the Hiberno-British metallurgical industry. We have already cited the numbers of parallels that exist between some of the Irish Passage Grave material and material from the Wessex

Bronze Age culture of southern Britain, and quoted Mr
T. G. E. Powell's views of the Boyne tombs as being largely
contemporary 'with Mycenaean civilisation and the High
Bronze Age of Middle Europe'. Powell means by this phrase
'the High Bronze Age' the period between 1550 and 1300 B.C.,
when there were 'a series of interdependent and chronologically
overlapping cultures' in trans-Alpine Europe all with skilled
craftsmen working in bronze. One of these was the Armorican
Bronze Age culture of Brittany, another the Wessex culture,
and a third the Irish Bronze Age culture which he refers to as
the Boyne culture, a name which has been adopted by Professor Grahame Clark in his *World Prehistory* (Cambridge,
1961, 140). Powell stresses the Wessex-Mycenaean elements in
the culture of the Boyne tombs and links together monuments
like Cueva de Romeral at Antequera in southern Spain, Ile
Longue in southern Brittany and New Grange itself, seeing
them as tombs of chieftains of these High Bronze Age societies.

There is nothing incompatible here with what we have
already said ourselves. New Grange may be as late as 1600 to
1300 B.C. We think not, at present. We see the Passage Graves
of Ireland as the tombs of people who first colonized Ireland
from Iberia somewhere perhaps around 3000 B.C., who certainly had a knowledge of copper-working in their homeland,
and who lived on into the middle of the second millennium
B.C. and were responsible for the development of the Irish
High Bronze Age. This is not really an instance of having your
cake and eating it. It seems to us at present that this is the only
explanation of those archaeological facts which we now have.

We have said that the total number of Passage Graves in
Ireland is somewhere between a hundred and fifty and two
hundred. The total number of megalithic tombs in Ireland is
well over a thousand. The total number of Passage Graves in
the British Isles is in the region of two hundred and fifty and
there are in the British Isles about two thousand megalithic

tombs. What is the relation of the Passage Graves to other varieties of megalithic tomb in Ireland and elsewhere in the British Isles? This is a big question, but it is immediately relevant to our purpose in this book. Unless it is answered we cannot assess the importance of the tombs in the Bend of the Boyne. To put the issue bluntly: Are the Boyne tombs the beginning of all megalithic architecture in the British Isles or are the Irish Passage Graves just one of many variant groups derived from different parts of the continent?

It is customary to distinguish four groups among the Irish megalithic monuments as follows: (1) *the Passage Graves*, with some aspects of which this book has been concerned; (2) *the Court Cairns*; (3) *the Wedge-shaped Gallery Graves*; (4) *the Portal Dolmens*. This is the basic classification used in Dr Raftery's *Prehistoric Ireland*, in *Antiquities of the Irish Countryside* written by Professor ÓRíordáin, and again recently in volume one of the *Survey of the Megalithic Tombs of Ireland* by Professor de Valera and Sean ÓNuallain (Dublin, 1961). We should like a distinction to be made between Passage Graves of the Boyne–Loughcrew–Carrowkeel–Carrowmore type and the small V-shaped Passage Graves or Entrance Graves which occur in the Tramore district of County Waterford; and we do not believe these small Passage Graves are derived from the Boyne tombs in Ireland but are connected with similar monu-ments in the Isles of Scilly and the Channel Islands—all three probably representing settlements from western Brittany. Apart from this small point, our question is: What direct relation have the Boyne Passage Graves with the Court Cairns of Ire-land, the Wedge-shaped Gallery Graves, and the Portal Dolmens?

We do not like the word dolmen because it has so many different usages, but the term Portal-Dolmen is now used very extensively in the literature on Irish megaliths. We would prefer to call these monuments Portal-Chambers. They are rectangular or wedge-shaped chambers which frequently possess a pair of large matched uprights supporting the chamber but also form-ing a portal and emphasizing the entrance. These portal cham-bers are mainly found in eastern Ireland; some of them are very impressive indeed—the capstone of the chamber at Browne's Hill, County Carlow has been estimated as weighing 100 tons. Portal-Chambers are also found across the Irish Sea in Corn-wall and in Wales. There seems to be no case for connecting these Portal-Chambers in any way with the Passage Graves; they must represent another element in the megalithic coloniza-tion of the British Isles.

The same must surely be true for the Wedge-shaped Gallery Graves. There are about four hundred of these in Ireland; in-deed Professor de Valera has described them as 'undoubtedly the most numerous and widely dispersed megalithic tomb type in Ireland'. In plan they seem to have no connections whatso-ever with the Passage Graves; the evidence for their date is slight, but we agree with de Valera when he says, 'It is not rash to suggest a date probably straddling the middle of the second millennium B.C.' There remain the Court Cairns which are mainly concentrated in the north and north-west of Ireland and consist of a central or terminal court leading into one or more rectangular chambers. It has been suggested that the plan of a monument with a central court might have developed out of a Passage Grave and that these open central courts in the monuments of northern Ireland could be developments from earlier megalithic tombs in the same way as the great Maltese megalithic temples developed out of earlier megalithic tombs and rock-cut tombs. It must also be remembered that one of the sites at Carrowkeel—site E—is in a long cairn such as is the standard shape of the mound in all the Court Cairns. But neither this single example of a long cairn in a Passage Grave cemetery nor the hypothesis of the evolution of the court with chambers out of a Passage Grave are convincing arguments to connect the Passage Graves with the Court Cairns. It looks then as if, so far as Ireland is concerned, the megalithic monu/ments may represent five separate groups of people severally responsible for the Boyne Passage Graves, the Tramore En/trance Graves, the Court Cairns, the Wedge/shaped Gallery Graves, and the Portal/Chambers.

Granted this is so for Ireland, our next question must be: Where did these other groups come from? If we agree as most archaeologists do that the Irish Passage Graves come from southern Spain and Portugal, and that the Passage Grave builders of Iberia were one of the most important elements in the origin of megalithic tombs, we must ask whether in some areas outside Ireland—in Iberia, or France, or Britain—Passage Graves may not have developed into other types of monument which were ancestral to the Tramore Entrance Graves, the Court Cairns, the Wedge/shaped Gallery Graves and the Portal/Chambers. Is it possible that these classes of tombs stand in Ireland in a cousinly relationship to the great Boyne tombs?

Let us look at Great Britain first. The megalithic tombs in England, Wales and Scotland are of many types. There are the Passage Graves which we have already discussed as parts of the Boyne Passage Grave Group, and there are the tombs in south/west Cornwall and the Isles of Scilly which are Entrance Graves and to be connected with the Tramore and Breton tombs of this type. Then there exist in Kent a few tombs be/longing to what is usually referred to as the Medway Group which seem to be connected with megalithic monuments in Holland. Apart from these groups, most of the megalithic tombs of England, Wales and Scotland are in long cairns and some of them bear at least superficial resemblances to some of the Court Cairns of northern Ireland. They are usually referred to as the Solway–Clyde tombs and the Severn–Cotswold tombs; we would prefer to regard them as one group under the name of the Clyde–Severn tombs. Now, it is perfectly true that there are many monuments in the southern aspect of the Clyde–Severn group that present a superficial resemblance to the Cruciform Passage Graves of Ireland. These monuments are in South Wales and the Cotswolds and have been labelled by one of us (G.E.D.) 'Transepted Gallery Graves'. Characteristic sites are Parc le Breos Cwm in Glamorgan, Hetty Pegler's Tump and Notgrove in Gloucestershire, Stoney Littleton in Somerset, and West Kennet in Wiltshire. It is our belief that these monuments and associated ones in the south, west Midlands of Britain and in south-east Wales were derived from tombs in southern Brittany and the Vendée and gave rise to the Clyde–Solway tombs and the Court Cairns of northern Ireland. It is therefore of importance here to consider the view of the late Professor Gordon Childe, who asked us all to consider seriously whether the Transepted Gallery Graves of Britain could not have been derived from the Irish Cruciform Passage Graves. We could therefore have a curious lineage beginning with the Irish Passage Graves and passing through the Severn–Cotswold tombs to the Court Cairns of northern Ireland. It is indeed still quite arguable that the Irish Cruciform Passage Graves were married to the idea of long wedge-shaped cairns in southern Britain and that modified versions of this plan spread up the Irish Sea to south-west Scotland and northern Ireland.

We do not, however, think this is the correct explanation. The Severn–Cotswold tombs, and their descendants the Clyde–Carlingford Court Cairns represent a direct settlement of Britain from the continent in the same way as do the Irish Passage Graves. Our question then arrives in its final form: Are the Irish Passage Graves apparented to monuments in Iberia which themselves may be the parents of the Transepted Gallery Graves in western France from which the Severn-Cotswold tombs sprang? The honest answer to this is that in the present state of our knowledge of megalithic architecture in Western Europe, we do not know, but it may well be so. For many years we have thought of megalithic architecture in terms of a dichotomy—the Passage Graves on the one hand and the Gallery Graves or *allées couvertes* on the other. This clear dichotomy was adumbrated by Gordon Childe and developed by Daniel, but at present it seems perhaps an over-simplification of a very complicated problem. There certainly appear in Ireland and France and Scandinavia two very different types of megalithic tomb, the Passage Grave and the Gallery Grave; in distribution and chronology and grave goods too they seem different. The real question is the origin of the long stone tomb, the Gallery Grave or *allée couverte*. It has been argued that it started in southern France as the translation of a long rock-cut tomb into a surface megalithic structure, that this long megalithic structure, with its supporting and covering elongated cairn spread up into western France, and that here it developed a standard pattern of paired side chambers which produced the Transepted Gallery Grave of the Vendée and the Loire-Atlantique and the Morbihan which eventually spread to the British Isles. On this thesis we could regard the Irish megalithic monuments as the results of two separate streams from the Mediterranean, both starting with the rock-cut and dry-walled tombs of Iberia and southern France: the idea of the Irish Passage Graves came from southern Iberia, the idea of the Irish Court Cairns and Wedge-shaped Galleries came ultimately from southern France via Brittany and England.

But this hypothesis of the dual nature of the megalithic colonization of north-western Europe may not merely be an over-simplification—it may be quite wrong. In the south of Spain and in south Portugal we can distinguish a typological series developing from normal classical Passage Graves through V-shaped Passage Graves to *allées couvertes* or Gallery Graves, and while this typology cannot be supported (or disproved) by archaeological evidence, it does lead from an agreed intrusive type. It is thus theoretically possible to derive the Gallery Graves of Western Europe from southern Iberia, or, as Daniel has argued, to regard the form of megalithic collective tomb which we label as a Gallery Grave as a morphological type invented in several areas—southern Iberia, southern France, and perhaps Scandinavia. In the present state of our knowledge of the archaeology of megalithic monuments it is certainly arguable that some, or possibly all, of the Gallery Graves of France and the British Isles are derived from the Gallery Graves of southern Iberia.

We could then see the original colonists as spreading from southern Iberia to France and the British Isles, with the Passage Grave as the tomb of their chiefs, and later variants of this form spreading at later dates; the Gallery Grave from southern Iberia would be one of these and the V-Passage Grave of Iberia and Brittany another. Indeed there is a very strong case for seeing groups from Iberia settling in Brittany and in the Paris Basin and introducing among the indigenous population there (the mixture of Mesolithic and Neolithic people which, when they were building tombs, were called by Bosch-Gimpera and Serra Rafols, the Seine–Oise–Marne people) the custom of building long megalithic tombs. The art on the Paris Basin tombs and on the Breton Gallery Graves, while it has been compared with the figure of goddesses on the statues-menhirs of southern France, compares even more closely with the art on idols in south Iberian tombs, with the art on pots—the *symbol-keramik*—and the art occasionally found on Iberian tombs like that on the Dolmen de Soto. Then there have been found in south-western Iberia, and described by the Leisners, tombs at El Pozuelo which are remarkably like the so-called Transepted Gallery Graves of north-western France and the Severn–Cotswold area.

This is not the place to go into the origins and interrelations of the French chamber tombs. All we are concerned with here is to discuss the possibility that the Severn–Cotswold tombs (and therefore, if our argument about their relationship with the Clyde–Carlingford tombs is correct, the Court Cairns of Ireland) might ultimately come from Iberia, via Brittany, and that the people who planned and built and were buried in these tombs may be latter-day Passage Grave people. This would, if we accept the C 14 chronology of the Breton Passage Graves, make the Passage Grave builders the earliest of the megalith folk in Ireland and the builders of all the other types of tomb later collaterals of theirs. There is still at the back of the writing of many archaeologists today the idea that the long barrows and Court Cairns of the British Isles are 'Neolithic' and early, while the round barrows with Passage Graves are 'Copper and Bronze Age' and later. But this is really founded on very little evidence, and, as we have seen, the use of phrases like Neolithic, Copper Age and Bronze Age are not really helpful or meaningful ones in a true chronological sense. These interrelations are issues which the next generation of archaeo-logists in Ireland will solve.

There is, however, one general issue which cannot be solved in isolation in Ireland itself. We have described how the tombs built and used by the Aegean colonists in Iberia were either rock-cut or dry-walled with corbel roofs, but that there are also large numbers of morphologically analogous tombs which are entirely megalithic in construction in Iberia, that the majority of analogous tombs in the British Isles are megalithic, and all the analogous tombs in Scandinavia, north-west Germany and north Holland are megalithic. There are no dry-walled and corbel-vaulted tombs in the Scandinavian–north German–Dutch area. What is the explanation of this? How is it that the East-Mediterranean-inspired form of collective tomb, which did not use megaliths, began to do so in Iberia, and eventually used megaliths to the exclusion of the original colonial tech-niques? This is a large and general question involving all aspects of megalithic theory, but it cannot be left untouched here since New Grange and the other tombs in the Bend of the Boyne are, constructionally, monuments that combine megali/ thic and non/megalithic collective tomb architecture. And it should be emphasized that even the corbelling at New Grange deserves the word megalithic; it is not the neatly built corbel/ ling of small stones set together dry as at Alcalá.

Many explanations have been given for the rise of megalithic architecture in the Mediterranean and in Western and Northern Europe. We need only consider here three main theories; these we propose to call the *geological*, the *technical*, and the *indigenous tradition* theories. The *geological* theory suggests that when people who were accustomed to constructing tombs on the surface with dry walling and corbel roofs or underground by cutting into the living rock moved to areas where the rock could not be easily cut in this way and small stones were not readily available for building walls and vaults, they looked around for other sources of building materials and turned to the use of large stones as walls and flat roofs. This is really an argument for geographical or geological determinism. We certainly seem to have one example in the British Isles of such geological control. It seems very likely that the Passage Grave builders moved from Ireland and Wales up to western Scotland; the builders of monuments like Maes Howe, then, are descendants or col/ laterals of the builders of New Grange. In Maes Howe itself we have a monument which is built of small stones carefully fitted together, and this may well be (as in the case of the village of Skara Brae) a direct result of the availability of rock that splits easily into small pieces.

The *technical* theory argues that when the custom of cutting tombs in the rock or of building dry/walled and corbel/vaulted tombs on the surface spread among the indigenous people in Iberia, or when the technical competence of the original colonists failed, they adopted a simpler way of construction, namely the use of large stones for walling and roofing. The *indigenous tradition* theory is one that has been canvassed for some while in Iberian archaeology and revived recently by the Leisners. It suggests that the native 'Neolithic' people of Portugal and north-western Spain, who existed before the arrival of Aegean colonists, had themselves invented megalithic architecture locally and buried their dead, not necessarily collectively, in square and polygonal megalithic single chambers; and that when the Aegean colonists arrived with their foreign ideas and techniques, including collective burial in Passage Graves, worship of a Mother-Goddess with a special funerary iconography, and a knowledge of copper-working, the natives, adopting some of these customs, evolved the megalithic Passage Grave which was a compromise between, and a fusion of, the two traditions. Indeed the Leisners suggest that the megalithic Passage Grave might have evolved separately as a copy of the colonists' tombs, and they cite two examples in the Reguengos area of east Portugal—Anta 2 da Commenda 36 and Anta 1 of Farisoa III—where dry-walled corbel-vaulted tombs were inserted in round mounds which already contained orthostatic Passage Graves and were therefore later than these. However, this evidence, and also the evidence from Barnenez South in north Brittany, of a corbel-vaulted tomb being built later than a megalithic tomb, does not prove that the *indigenous tradition* theory always applies.

At the moment it does not seem to us that we have the evidence to decide on this general issue of the evolution of tomb types in prehistoric Europe. We need a series of Carbon 14 dates from megalithic and non-megalithic sites to resolve our difficulties. But what we can say is that in Ireland, that is to say as far as the Ireland of the builders of Passage Graves is concerned, both sets of techniques—megalithic and dry-walled—came together and are indeed combined in a most remarkable way in New Grange to provide a major prehistoric work.

Any further discussion of the interrelations of collective tombs and megaliths in Ireland and Western Europe in general would take us beyond the scope of the present book. We feel we have now set New Grange and the other tombs in the Bend of the Boyne in the historical perspective that we think is their rightful one. Thus, in our present way of thinking, we brush away the Druids, the 'little people', the Egyptians, the lost tribes of Israel, the Danes, and Mithras. We see New Grange and the other Passage Graves of the British Isles as tombs (and perhaps also cult shrines or temples) of important chiefs of prospecting and trading communities who came from Iberia first of all in the end of the fourth millennium B.C. and who traded and voyaged backwards and forwards along the Atlantic seaways for fifteen hundred years or more, and as a direct result of whose voyages of exploration and trade there eventually developed the metallurgical industry of Ireland at the end of the third millennium B.C.

We have said 'historical perspective', but we are not forget-ting that we are dealing with prehistory and that when we try to give reality in terms of people and behaviour to analyses of forms and distributions we are going outside the archaeological record. Yet, unless occasionally this is done and the controlled historical imagination of the archaeologist is allowed to guess at what lies behind his typologies and distributions, we are doomed to an arid archaeology and books full of phrases like, 'Alas, we cannot answer that question' and 'Oh, dear, if we only knew!' Many people have made this jump over the reasonable limits of interpretation in trying to explain the role of the Passage Grave builders in European history. Elliot Smith and Perry saw them as Children of the Sun wandering from Egypt. Wheeler has seen them as travelling undertakers, and Gordon Childe as saints and missionaries. We see them as Iberian traders and prospectors imbued with a religious faith and practising a special form of burial.

A most notable attempt at recreating the historical back-ground of prehistoric events has recently been made by Geoffrey Bibby in his *Four Thousand Years Ago* (1962), where he paints a picture of the merchant adventurers of the western seaways which is clearer and more historical than what we have said. He sees large ships from Crete and the Aegean setting out to Iberia but also going on to the British Isles and Scandinavia. 'They were', he writes, 'part traders and part prospectors, these wide-ranging sea captains. But though they scarcely realised it, they were most to make their mark as missionaries.' Bibby sees the ships with crews not entirely Cretan, but manned with men drawn from the islands of the Aegean and scattered cities on the coast of Asia Minor like Troy. He thinks they may not have been Cretan-owned but that 'it is probable that the western trade was financed by merchants from the whole of the Aegean.' He sees the whole process as the establishment of may be 'not more than a Cretan factor, with two or three assistants, perhaps recruited from among the natives; or there might be two or three families of Aegeans, supplementing their trading by fishing and farming.' 'The ships from home,' he writes, 'calling in two or three times a year, would land supplies and trade goods, and take on board such local products as the factor had collected since the last visit.' He sees these Aegean factors moving along the Atlantic seaways—whereas we have rather envisaged Aegeanized Iberians as controlling the Atlan-tic end of this trade—and asks that we should not expect to find Aegean and East Mediterranean objects in British, Irish and Scandinavian tombs, saying that in any long voyage such as from the Mediterranean to New Grange, Maes Howe and Jutland, there would be 'several complete turnovers of cargo'.

Bibby has gone further than we have done, and deliberately so because he is trying to get across to the general reader the historical implications of archaeological facts; but the general thesis is the same. As we stand outside New Grange looking at

the decorated entrance stones (and, as we hope, the other decorated stones of the kerb which will be revealed to us in the next
few years), or walk into the great stone tomb with its splendid
roof more than four thousand years old and its great decorated
stones; as we lie in the cold stone basin in the north side chamber and look up at the wonderfully decorated capstone with its
goddess-faces in various forms of schematization; and as we
stand outside the great tomb and, on top of it, look around at
the other tombs and monuments in the Bend of the Boyne, we
must have a feeling of the great past of Ireland, and a sense that
we are in the very middle of one of the great centres of Iberian
or possibly Aegean settlement in ancient times. We do not
believe that the Irish ever forgot their debt to and kinship with
these Mediterreanean people. We believe that the great men
buried in New Grange and elsewhere were always great figures
in early historic Ireland and that that is why, for example,
Christian Tara developed on the site of a pagan cemetery. New
religions for old: Tara is an example of one Mediterranean
religion replacing another, and we remember the other remarkable sites in Western Europe where megalithic tombs have
actually been incorporated into functioning Christian churches
—Gangas de Onis near Oviedo, for example, or the Chapelle
des Septs-Saints in the Côtes-du-Nord of Brittany. To cite these
examples is not to insist on continuity; it is to suggest that, unlike England, where there is no continuing tradition of the
past from say Stonehenge and Avebury into historic times—
except for the memories enshrined in Geoffrey of Monmouth
—the megalithic past of Ireland might well have been a living
memory, though not, *pace* Dr Raftery, a living practice in
Roman times, and the times of St Patrick. It is also to suggest
that the Passage Grave builders, the men of New Grange and
the Bend of the Boyne, were and are, a very important element
in the many ethnic elements that make up the Irish people of
History.

Bibliographical Note

Here is a short list of books and articles on which some of the statements in this book are based, and which are suitable for further reading. This is only a selection; for further sources which are not detailed here, see particularly the entries marked with an asterisk. The following abbreviations have been used:

JRSAI   *Journal of the Royal Society of Antiquaries of Ireland* (Dublin)
PPS   *Proceedings of the Prehistoric Society* (Cambridge)
PRIA(C)   *Proceedings of the Royal Irish Academy*, Series C (Dublin)

George Coffey's dates were 1857 to 1916: an obituary of him will be found in JRSAI, 1917, 96, where we read of his 'striking presence, flexible intelligence, fine mental quality and power of lucid and eloquent exposition' which 'made him a notable figure'. His articles on 'The Origin of Prehistoric Ornament in Ireland' appeared in PRIA (C), volumes XXIV (1894), 349, XXV (1895), 195, XXVI (1896), 34 and XXVII (1897), 28; they formed the basis of his book *New Grange (Brugh na Boine) and other Incised Tumuli in Ireland, the influence of Crete and the Aegean in the extreme west of Europe in early times* (Dublin, 1912). Also relevant here is his *The Bronze Age in Ireland* (Dublin, 1913).

Since Coffey wrote, there has been no new book on New Grange but it and the other sites in the Bend of the Boyne have been discussed in general books on early Ireland such as R. A. S. Macalister, *Ireland in Pre-Celtc Times* (Dublin and London, 1921); and *The Archaeology of Ireland* (Dublin and London, 1928). This latter came out in a revised and rewritten second edition in 1949: the 1949 edition should be used with caution. Wood-Martin's *Pagan Ireland* (London, 1895) and his *Traces of the Elder Faiths of Ireland* (London, 1902), while out-of-date, are still useful, and are well illustrated. For modern surveys of Irish prehistory see A. Mahr's 'New Aspects and Problems in Irish Prehistory', *PPS*, 1937, 261; J. Raftery, *Prehistoric Ireland* (London, 1951); *ÓRíordáin, Antiquities of the Irish Countryside* (London, 1942, 1943 and revised and reset third edition, 1953), and Chapter Nine, 'Archaeology', in J.

Meenan and D. A. Webb, *A View of Ireland* (British Association for the Advancement of Science, Dublin, 1957).

For the general background of the prehistory of the British Isles, see V. G. Childe, *Prehistoric Communities of the British Isles* (London and Edinburgh, 1940); S. Piggott, *British Prehistory* (1949); J. G. D. Clark, *Prehistoric England* (revised edition, 1963); J. and C. F. C. Hawkes, *Prehistoric Britain* (Penguin Books, 1943); and as detailed regional studies, J. F. S. Stone, *Wessex* (London, 1958) and R. Rainbird Clarke, *East Anglia* (London, 1960).

For the prehistory of Scotland, see V. G. Childe, *The Prehistory of Scotland* (London, 1935); S. Piggott (ed.), *The Prehistoric Peoples of Scotland* (London, 1962): and of Wales, I. Ll. Foster and Glyn Daniel (ed.), *Prehistoric and Early Wales* (London, 1964). For the general background of European prehistory, see V. G. Childe, *The Dawn of European Civilisation* (sixth edition, London, 1957) and *Prehistoric Migrations in Europe* (Oslo, 1950); C. F. C. Hawkes, *The Prehistoric Foundations of Europe to the Mycenean Age* (London, 1940); T. G. E. Powell, 'Barbarian Europe', Chapter XII of S. Piggott (ed.), *The Dawn of Civilisation* (London, 1961).

On the Boyne tombs, in addition to Coffey, see Leask, 'Inscribed Stones recently discovered at Dowth Tumulus, Co. Meath', PRIA C, XL (1932-4), 162; R. A. S. Macalister, 'A Preliminary Report on the Excavation of Knowth', PRIA(C), XLIX (1943), 131; ÓRíordáin, 'Unrecorded Earthwork near New Grange', JRSAI, 1954, 93; P. J. Hartnett, JRSAI, 1954, 181; and G. Eogan, 'A Neolithic Habitation Site and Megalithic Tomb in Townleyhall Townland, Co. Louth', JRSAI, 1963, 37 and 'A New Passage Grave in Co. Meath', *Antiquity*, 1963, 226.

The beginning of modern studies on Irish Passage Graves dates from the publication of T. G. E. Powell's paper, *'The Passage Graves of Ireland' in PPS, 1938, 239. The art was studied by Breuil and Macalister in their 'A Study of the Chronology of Bronze Age RockSculpture in Ireland', PRIA(C), 1921, 6, and 'Les Pétroglyphes d'Irlande', *Revue Archéologique*, 1921, 75, and more recently, by Eoin MacWhite in his *'A New View on Irish BronzeAge Rockscribings', JRSAI, 1946, 60. Powell and MacWhite contain all the major references to Irish Passage Graves and Irish Megalithic Art, but see also the following, published since they wrote: M. J. O'Kelly, 'An Example of Passage Grave Art from County Cork', *Journal of the Cork Historical and Archaeological Society*, 1949, 8; P. J. Hartnett, 'Excavation of a Passage Grave at Fourknocks, County Meath', PRIA(C), LVIII (1957), 197; Etienne Rynne, 'Survey of a Probable Passage Grave Cemetery at Bremore, County Dublin', JRSAI, 1960, 79, and 'The Decorated Stones at Seefin', JRSAI, 1963, 85; A. E. P. Collins and D. M. Waterman, *Millin Bay; a Late Neolithic Cairn in County Down* (Belfast, 1955), and 'Knockmany Chambered Grave, County Tyrone', *Ulster Journal of Archaeology*, 1952, 26, this latter to be read in conjunction with George Coffey's 'Knockmany', in PRIA(C), XXVIII, 1898, 93.

On Irish megaliths in general, W. C. Borlase, *The Dolmens of Ireland* (London, 1897), an old work but still valuable; Wood-Martin, *The Rude Stone Monuments of Ireland* (Dublin, 1888); R. de Valera, 'The Court Cairns of Ireland', PRIA(C), 1960, 9; R. de Valera and S. Ó Nualláin, *Survey of the Megalithic Tombs of Ireland: Vol. I: County Clare* (Dublin, 1961).

On megalithic monuments and associated cultures in Western Europe, see S. Piggott, *The Neolithic Cultures of the British Isles* (Cambridge, 1954); P. R. Giot, *Brittany* (London, 1960); G. E. Daniel, *The Prehistoric Chamber Tombs of England and Wales* (Cambridge, 1950), *The Megalith Builders of Western Europe* (London, 1958; revised edition Penguin Books, 1963), *The Prehistoric Chamber Tombs of France* (London, 1960); A. S. Henshall, *The Chambered Tombs of Scotland*, Vol. I (Edinburgh, 1963); G. and V. Leisner, *Die Megalithgräber der Iberischen Halbinsel* (Berlin, 1943 and 1956); and Pericot y Garcia, *Los Sepulcros Megaliticos Catalanes y la Cultura Pirenaica* (1950).

On megalithic art in general, see H. Breuil's Presidential Address to the Prehistoric Society of East Anglia, printed in its *Proceedings* for 1934 (289), and his *Les Peintures Rupestres Schématiques de la Péninsule Ibérique* (Paris, 1933); T. G. E. Powell and G. E. Daniel, *Barclodiad y Gawres* (Liverpool, 1956), J. L. Forde-Johnston, 'Megalithic Art in the North-west of Britain: The Calderstones, Liverpool', PPS, 1957, 20; E. Octobon, 'Statues-menhirs, stèles gravées, dalles sculptées', *Revue Anthropologique*, 1931, 299; M. Péquart, St-J. Péquart, and Z. le Rouzic, *Corpus des signes gravés des monuments mégalithiques du Morbihan* (Paris, 1927). There are also several general books dealing with those aspects of

megalithic art which portray a goddess figure; such are O. G. S. Craw,
ford, *The Eye Goddess* (London, 1957); S. van Cles-Reden, *The Realm
of the Great Goddess* (London, 1961), and G. Stacul, *La Grande Madre*
(Rome, 1963). All are well illustrated, but the text of the first two should
be treated with caution.

Travel Note

The centre for visiting New Grange is Slane, a small village 28 miles
from Dublin and 9 miles from Drogheda (Ordnance Survey Map one
inch sheet 91 and half inch sheet 13). There are buses from the bus centre
in Dublin, and in the tourist season special trips take in New Grange.
For full information write to the Irish Tourist Bureau in London
(19 Regent Street, London, S.W.1) or Dublin (14 Upper O'Connell
Street). A small site museum was installed at New Grange in 1964. All
visitors to the sites in the Bend of the Boyne should also, on returning to
Dublin, visit the National Museum in Kildare Street which has a superb
collection of Irish Antiquities as well as departments dealing with Art
and Industry, and Natural History. The Irish Tourist Bureau publishes
an illustrated guide to the counties of Ireland. See also the *Blue Guide to
Ireland* and the *Shell Guide to Ireland* by Lord Killanin and M. V.
Duignan. *Antiquities of the Irish Countryside*, by S. P. ÓRíordáin, has
already been mentioned in the Bibliographical Note.

Sources of Illustrations

The plates are made from photographs taken (or owned) by the following, whose copyright they are:

Professor S. P. ÓRíordáin: 1, 2, 3, 4, 7, 8, 9, 10, 14, 15, 18, 19, 23, 25, 26, 27, 33, 34, 35, 50, 52, 55, 60, 61, 63, 66, 68

P. Danagher: 11, 21

T. H. Mason and Sons: 28, 43, 56, 57, 67

Dr J. K. St Joseph and the Cambridge University Collection of Air Photographs: 36, 37, 38, 51, 52, 53, 54

The Royal Irish Academy: 48, 49

Bord Fáilte Eireann: 5, 12, 13, 16, 17, 20, 22, 24, 29, 30, 31, 32, 39, 40, 42, 44, 45, 46, 47

The National Monuments Branch of the Commissioners of Public Works in Ireland: 58, 59, 62, 64

Professor M. J. O'Kelly: 65, 69

Musée des Antiquités Nationales, St. Germain-en-Laye: 70

P. A. Clayton: 6

THE PLATES

3

4

13

14

23

24

25

26

27

31

32

33

34

37

38

39

40

43

44

45

46

48

49

50

51

52

53

54

55

56

57

58

59

60

61

62

63

64

67

68

Notes on the Plates

1 New Grange. The barrow photographed from the air in 1956 before the felling of the trees. It is 280 feet in diameter by 40 feet high and covers about an acre of ground.

2 New Grange. The barrow from the ground.

3 New Grange. Three of the stones of the free-standing circle of menhirs surrounding New Grange. The tallest of these is 8 feet high.

4 New Grange. The construction of the barrow showing the quartz pebbles with which it was originally surfaced.

5 New Grange. The decorated false lintel with its pattern of halved lozenges in relief, set above the entrance to the burial chamber.

6 New Grange. The decorated stone at the entrance to the burial chamber. It is in line with and part of the kerb circle of stones. This stone with its pocked pattern of spirals and lozenges is one of the most famous examples of mural megalithic art in Europe.

7 New Grange. Looking up the passage from the entrance. At the entrance itself the passage is 3 feet wide by 5 feet high.

8 New Grange. Half-way up the passage, which is 62 feet long, and looking in towards the chamber. This photograph shows orthostat R.12 with its decoration of parallel shallow grooves or channels.

9 New Grange. A view down the passage from the central chamber.

10 New Grange. The corbelled roof of the central chamber. The chamber is 8 to 10 feet across and its height is 19 feet 6 inches. This is the best preserved corbelled vault from any prehistoric chamber tomb in western and west Mediterranean Europe.

11 New Grange. The south side chamber with a large stone basin 3 feet 6 inches across.

12 New Grange. The two stone basins in the north side chamber. The lower, flatter one is 6 feet across, the upper one is 3 feet 6 inches by 4 feet, and has a design of two hollows (probably a face motif) on its western edge. (See p. 62.)

13, 14 New Grange. Two photographs of stone R.18, to show the technique of decoration. Plate 14 shows the marks of a toothed chisel—the prehistoric equivalent of the claw tool of the modern worker in stone.

15 New Grange. Decoration of the stone (C.3) at the back of the south side chamber.

16 New Grange. Three spirals, combined to form a triskele figure, on orthostat C.10 in the western side chamber. The small spiral of the three is uppermost, and the top of this stone is to the left. The photograph is printed this way to show clearly the technique of pocking the designs.

17 New Grange. Detail of the decoration on stone L.19. This pattern of spirals and lozenges shows very well the details of the pocked technique of decoration.

18 New Grange. General view of decoration on stone L.19.

19 New Grange. Stone R.21 showing details of the ribbon or ribbed dressing of the stone. (See p. 53.)

20 New Grange. Stone L.22 with designs of pocked chevrons and triangles.

21 New Grange. Stone C.16 with design of lozenges and triangles on the edge of the stone facing towards the centre of the chamber.

22 New Grange. Decoration near the top of stone R.21 consisting of halved lozenges, alternate halves being pocked.

23   New Grange. The back stone (C.3) of the southern side chamber, decorated with three spirals. For detail of the central spiral see plate 15.

24   New Grange. The pocked motif on stone C.4 of the southern side chamber (? fern-leaf, ? palm-branch), often referred to as a fir-tree or fir-tree man. Perhaps a highly schematized human figure? (See pp. 60 and 116.)

25   New Grange. Motif on stone C.4 in the southern side chamber, described by Colonel Vallancey as Ogham writing, by Governor Pownall as Phoenician writing and by George Coffey as a ship. (See p. 59.)

26   New Grange. Decorated corbel above C.2 in the southern side chamber; an attractively composed linear pattern of eleven lozenges and zigzags.

27   New Grange. Stone C.2 in the southern side chamber, decorated with a spiral above which are five lozenges and two triangles.

28   New Grange. General view of the decoration on the underside of the capstone in the north side chamber. This stone, some of the decoration of which is seen in detail in plates 29 and 30, is, together with the three decorated stones in the kerb (Coffey's *a*, *b*, and *c*), among the most famous examples of megalithic art in Ireland.

29, 30   New Grange. Details of some of the decoration on the underside of the capstone of the north side chamber. (For a general view of the whole design see plate 28, and fig. 11.) At the bottom of plate 29 can be clearly seen the face motif (or oculi motif) representing the Eye-Goddess or Funerary Goddess. Compare plate 61 (Knockmany).

31   New Grange. Decoration on the edge of stone over C.14.

32   New Grange. Decoration of pocked lozenges on edge of stone over C.15.

33   New Grange. Roof of passage, as seen when looking out from the centre of the chamber.

34 New Grange. Decoration of halved lozenges on corbel above stones R.20 and R.21.

35 New Grange. Decorated kerb-stone (Coffey's stone *b*) with opposed running spirals and lozenges and on the left a large pattern of pocked lozenges, halved lozenges and triangles.

36 Loughcrew. Air photograph of some of the Loughcrew tombs looking north-west. The carns in the foreground are, from right to left, K (50 feet in diameter), L (140 feet in diameter), and immediately north-west of it J (45 feet in diameter), H (55 feet in diameter), and I (65 feet in diameter). The top left quadrant of the photograph shows the largest of the Lough-crew carns, D, which is 200 feet in diameter, and comparable in size with New Grange, Dowth and Knowth. In front of it and in a line with H and L are G and F. Carn H, whose cruciform plan shows up clearly, is the site re-excavated by Dr Raftery and about the date of which there has been much discussion. (See pp. 122–4.)

37 Knowth. The barrow from the air. It is 225 feet in diameter by 40 to 50 feet in height (see pp. 73–7). Beyond is the smaller mound excavated by Dr G. Eogan (see p. 85 and fig. 21).

38 Dowth. The barrow from the air. It is 280 feet in diameter and 47 feet high. (See pp. 65–72.)

39 Dowth. Inside the south main chamber.

40 Dowth. The south chamber—entrance to the side chamber from the main chamber.

41 Dowth. The main, northern chamber: view looking down the passage. Note the decoration on the orthostats, and the stone basin.

42 Dowth. Detail of decoration in the north chamber.

43, 44 Detail of decorated stones in the kerb circle at Dowth.

45   Dowth. Entrance to the south chamber. Note the kerb-stones and the cup-marks on them.

46   Dowth. Outline plan of the monument laid out in white stones in modern times on the ground outside the monument. These stones are laid out to scale. The length of passage and chamber, from west to east, is just over 40 feet.

47   Dowth. North side chamber of northern chamber.

48, 49   Knowth. Decorated kerb-stones as revealed by Professor Macalister's excavations of 1943 (see pp. 74–7.) These and the other stones in the kerb circle are no longer visible to the visitor.

50   Tumulus B near New Grange. This mound is 90 feet in diameter and is on a flat expanse of land at the edge of the river Boyne, across which this photograph was taken. (P. 81 and the map, fig. 20.)

51   Earthwork near New Grange (site O on the map, fig. 20). This site was discovered by an air photographic reconnaissance in 1953. It is half a mile distant from New Grange. It consists of a large circular bank 120–150 yards in diameter; the maximum width of the bank measured, over its spread, about 60 yards. (See p. 87.)

52, 53   Circular earthworks, possibly henge monuments, north-west of New Grange (52), and north of Dowth (53).

54   Dowth. The large circular earthwork marked Q on the map (fig. 20). It has a diameter of between 420 and 450 feet, with openings on the south-west and north-east. (See p. 87.)

55   Sculptured stone made in 1956 by Mrs Gabriel Ó Ríordáin, using a quartz pebble on the same sort of stone as did the builders of New Grange, and copying motifs (at the same scale) from existing decorated stones at New Grange.

56, 57   Loughcrew. Decoration on the stones in the western side chamber of Loughcrew T.

58–60 Fourknocks I. Decorated lintels.

61 Knockmany. Decoration on the back stone of the chamber (Coffey's Stone *a*). Note the concentric circles and the face motif. The designs have been chalked in for easy recognition on the photograph. (See p. 24.)

62 Fourknocks I. Designs pocked on two of the uprights. (See p. 96.)

63 Seskillgreen. Decoration on one of the stones (also chalked in for photography).

64 Fourknocks I. Designs pocked on one of the uprights. (See p. 96.)

65 The decorated stone from Clear Island, County Cork. (See p. 99.)

66 Decorated stone from King's Mountain near Loughcrew. This stone, with its decoration in Irish Passage Grave style, may well have once been part of a chamber tomb.

67, 68 Decorated stones from tombs at Loughcrew.

69 Barclodiad y Gawres (Anglesey): Stone 22. The design pocked on this stone consists of a central panel of two vertically arranged lozenges each with a double outline. On each side of these central lozenges are zigzag lines springing from the side edges of the orthostat. Above the central lozenges and the flanking vertical zigzag lines is a band of horizontally running chevrons. Above this, the stone is badly weathered and has been much damaged by stone-breakers but there was a much-weathered spiral in the upper right-hand corner of the stone.

70 Decoration on one of the stones in the Passage Grave at Gavrinis (Morbihan), Brittany. This pocked art in southern Brittany, which includes spirals, is closely parallel with the art at New Grange.

Index

Alcalá, 23, 83, 130–1, 134, 138–9, 149

Alignments, 18

Allées couvertes, see Gallery Graves

Almizaraque, 131, 134

America, megaliths possibly in, 137

Annals of the Kingdom of Ireland by the Four Masters, 48

Annals of Ulster, 48

Anstis, John, 37, 38, 78

Antequera, 141

Arnal, J., 133

Atreus, Treasury of, 23

Aubrey, John, 30

Avebury, 21, 32, 153

Baltinglass, 93, 94

Barclodiad y Gawres, 71, 96, 99, 102, 104, 105, 117, 130

Barrows, 43–5

Bastions in settlements, 133–4

Bernabò Brea, L., 129–30, 132

Bibby, G., 152

Blance, B., 131–2

Borlase, W. C., 22, 45

Boyne, Battle of the, 15

Breuil, the Abbé H., 105, 111–17

Brugh na Boinne, 43–5

Bryn Celli Ddu, 102, 104, 129, 130

Burkitt, M. C., 111–13

Calderstones, The, 104–5

Canary Islands, 136

Carbon 14 dating, 120, and see Chrono‐logy of megaliths

Carn H, Loughcrew, see Loughcrew

Carnac, 18

Carnanmore, 93, 94, 102

Carrowkeel, 91, 92, 100, 110, 125

Carrowkeel ware, 90, 109–10, 125

Carrowmore, 91, 93, 94, 99, 100, 110

Cartailhac, E., 100

Channel Islands, 24

Childe, V. G., 90, 120, 145–6, 151, 155

Chisel, use of metal, 138

Chronology of megaliths, 25, 110, 118, 120–33

Clark, J. G. D., 141

Clark, R., 50, 52

Clava tombs, 106

Clear Island, Co. Cork, 99 and plate 65

Cloghlea, 88–9

Clonfinloch, 105

Clyde‐Carlingford tombs, 144–8, and see Court Cairns

Clyde‐Severn tombs, 144–5

Cocherel, 31, 34

Coffey, G., 12–14, 29, 39, 46, 51, 57–63, 66, 70–3, 80–9, 135, 154–5

Coins, Roman, 32, 41, 42

Collum, V. C. C., 122

Colt Hoare, Sir Richard, 41, 78

Conyngham, Lord Albert, 42

Conwell, E. A., 72, 101, 122–3

Court Cairns, 143–8

Crawford, O. G. S., 82, 113–14

Cromlechs, 22

Cyclades, 128

Cyprus, 126

Dean, Sir Thomas, 68
Déhus, 122, 127
De Paor, M. and L., 12
De Valera, R., 80, 97, 121, 142, 143
'Dolmens', 22, 23, 142
Dolmens of Ireland, The, see Borlase, W. C.
Dowth, 16, 19–21, 36, 50, 59, 65–72, 87–88, 110
Druids, 19, 33, 77, 88, 110
Dysse/Dös, 22

Earth-Mother Goddess, see Face motifs
Eday, 108, 116, 136
El Pozuelo, 147
Entrance Graves, 24
Eogan, G., 84, 89
Estridge, H., 45
Eye-goddess, see Face motifs

Face motifs, 62, 102, 105, 109, 114, 126–9, 131, 134
Faience beads, 125
Fergusson, J., 42
Folkton, chalk idols from, 109, 126
Food-vessels, 110, 125
Fourknocks (Four Knocks), 88, 91, 93, 94–7, 105, 117

Gallery Graves, 22, 24, 146–8
Gavrinis, 24, 51, 129, 135, and plate 70
Giant's Ring, Co. Down, 87
Glynn, F., 137
Gold ornaments at New Grange, 42
Grave goods, 109–11

Harristown, Co. Waterford, 125
Hartnett, P. J., 47, 94–6, 117

Hemp, W. J., 102
Hetty Pegler's Tump, 24, 145
Holm of Papa Westray, 106, 108, 126, 136

Ile Carn, 120
Ile Longue (Morbihan), 23, 24

Kercado (Morbihan), 120–1
Knockmany, 93, 94, 101, 102, 105, 126
Knowth, 16, 20–1, 36, 47, 64, 72–7, 86, 88

Langstone Rath, Co. Kildare, 87
La Tène art, 123–4
Leask, 47, 64, 76
Lébous (Hérault), 133, 139
Ledwich, E., 40–1
Leisner, G. and V., 127, 131, 147, 150
Lhwyd, E., 30–3, 38–9
Los Millares, 23, 127, 130–4, 138–9
Loughcrew, 91, 93, 94, 100–1
Loughcrew H., 13, 25, 122–4
Lough Gur, 88

Macalister, R. A. S., 19, 47, 49, 64, 73–7, 87, 100, 111–14, 123, 155
Maes Howe, 18, 21, 23, 106, 108, 134, 149
Mahr, A., 126, 155
Mallowan, M. E. L., 128, 129
Malta, 128–30, 133
Mané-Kernaplaye (Morbihan), 121
Megaliths, terminology of, 20–5
Mellaart, J., 129, 132
Menhir, 20
Metal and megaliths, 105, 133, 138–40, 148, and plate 14

Mgarr, see Malta
Millares, see Los Millares
Mitchell, F., 89
Molyneux, T., 34–6, 38–9
Monk Newton, 89
Mother-Goddess, see Face motifs
Mound of the Hostages, see Tara
Mycenae, 23, 43, 119, 129, 135

Netterville, the tea-house of Lord, 65, 77
Notgrove, 24, 145

Oculi ornament, see Face motifs
O'Donovan, J., 44, 48
ÓhEochaidhe, M., 47, 98
O'Kelly, M. J., 13, 14, 47, 49, 64
ÓRíordáin, Mrs. G., 14, and plate 55

Paris Basin, tombs in, 31
Passage Graves, 22, 24
Petrie, G., 43, 45
Petrology of New Grange, 50
Piggott, S., 114–17, 119
Portal-Chamber and Portal-Dolmen 23, 142–3
Powell, T. G. E., 98, 101, 113–14, 119–120, 141, 156–7

Radiocarbon dating, see Carbon 14 dating
Raftery, J., 25, 118–19, 122–4, 142, 153
Rathkenny, 105, 111
Rock-cut tombs, 25
Rowlands, the Reverend H., 33
Rügen, megaliths on island of, 91

Sardinia, 22, 128
Schist plaques, 111, 126, 127

Scilly-Tramore Group, 125, 144
Seefin, 94, 98
Seine-Oise-Marne, 147
Sept Iles, Les (Côtes-du-Nord), 120
Seskillgreen, 93, 94, 101
Settlement sites, 131, 133
Severn-Cotswold Group, 146–8
Ship motifs, 39–40, 59–60, 72
Ships, 135
Soto, Dolmen de, 127–8, 147
Souterrain, at Dowth, 74
Spirals, 61–2, 75, 94, 116, 119, 129
Statues-menhirs, 127–8, 147
Stonehenge, 18, 19, 21, 32, 53, 118, 153
Stone circles, 21
Symbolkeramik, 111, 127, 136, 147

Tara, 13, 15, 44, 59, 91, 93, 94, 97–8, 121, 125
Techniques of art, 52–3, and plates 13–17 and 55
Technique of stone preparation, 53–6, and plate 19
Tell Brak, 128–9
Tholoi, 23–4
Tibradden, 98
Topp, Mrs Celia, 42
Towneleyhall, 89–90
Transepted Gallery Graves, 24, 145–7
Tressé, 122
Troy, 128–9, 132

Valentinian, coin of Emperor, 32–3, 41
Vallancey, c., 38, 41, 59
Vila Nova de Sao Pedro, 131, 133
Vikings in Maes Howe, 106, 108
V-shaped Passage Graves, 24, 125

Wedge-shaped Gallery Graves, 24, 142–143

West Kennet, 24, 145

Wheeler, Sir Mortimer, 151

Wilde, Oscar, 16

Wilde, Sir William, 16, 29, 43–45, 59, 65–7, 71, 73, 84, 88

Wilkinson, G., 42–3, 49, 50

Wormius, O., 36

Worsaae, J. J. A., 43